PRAISE FOR
THE BRILLIANT
JERK CONUNDRUM

"Everything in this book rings true. All board members, CEOs, investors, and innovators should read it now. Epstein and Shelton make it clear what you need to create to protect the massive value that a brilliant, maverick leader can produce."

>—Phil Schlein, former CEO of Macy's California, former partner at U.S. Venture Partners, and former member of the board of directors at Apple for eight years

"For some [dominant visionaries], too much interference will stifle their ambition. For others, not interfering might allow them to go haywire and destroy the company. *The Brilliant Jerk Conundrum* shows how to tell the difference and what to do about it."

>—Srikant M. Datar, professor and senior associate dean at Harvard Business School and member of four boards

"In my 50 years as an executive and board member in Silicon Valley, I interacted with many brilliant jerks. I came within a whisker of joining the Theranos board and pulled out at the last minute. Disruptors can be unpredictable and unrealistic. You've captured how to navigate that challenge in this book."

—Dick Levy, former CEO and chairman of Varian

"Epstein and Shelton's book reminds boards that they must help CEOs to retain the ability to hear dissonant information and they must act swiftly and decisively when it becomes clear that the CEO has gone 'deaf.'"

—Jean-François Manzoni, president and Nestlé Chaired Professor at the International Institute for Management Development

"Silicon Valley is awash with leaders who actually aspire to be brilliant jerks like those profiled in this book. With Epstein and Shelton's guidance, board members, investors, and fellow employees will be ready to channel the brilliance without surrendering to the jerk."

—Kirk O. Hanson, Senior Lecturer Emeritus, Stanford Graduate School of Business

"*The Brilliant Jerk Conundrum* captures intriguing stories of how to generate and protect value when you have a rule-breaking trailblazer leading the charge."

—Krishna G. Palepu is the Ross Graham Walker Professor of Business Administration at Harvard Business School

THE
BRILLIANT
JERK
CONUNDRUM

THE BRILLIANT JERK CONUNDRUM

THRIVING WITH AND GOVERNING A DOMINANT VISIONARY

MARC J. EPSTEIN
and
ROB SHELTON

Published by The Conundrum Press, Palo Alto, California
Theconundrumpress.com

⟨ ⟩ GIRL FRIDAY
P R O D U C T I O N S

Edited and designed by Girl Friday Productions
girlfridayproductions.com

Cover design: Brad Foltz
Interior design: Paul Barrett

ISBN (paperback): 978-1-7339813-0-9
ISBN (hardcover): 978-1-7339813-2-3
ISBN (ebook): 978-1-7339813-1-6
Library of Congress Control Number: 2019905388
First edition

CONTENTS

INTRODUCTION

Look at lead news articles on any day, and you will likely find a story about a visionary CEO who has set out to change the business world. Some days the story is about a genius whose disruptive vision has created a dynamic new company successfully challenging the status quo. People are flocking to invest and aspiring to join the company to help make the vision a reality.

Other times, the story is about a genius CEO, apparently on course to change the world, who has suddenly gone haywire and done something weird, illegal, or just plain stupid. As a result, they damaged their company's value, scared investors, rankled employees, and gave the board of directors, who are responsible for governance, a major case of indigestion.

These stories raise a vital question: Before you trust and invest in or work for a company with a brainy CEO, how do you tell the difference between an inspired visionary winner such as Steve Jobs, a firebrand entrepreneur and sometimes jerk like Elon Musk at Tesla, and a time bomb like Elizabeth Holmes, who defrauded investors and imploded Theranos?

That's the conundrum. It seems impossible to know ahead of time what kind of creative genius you're betting on and, once you think you've figured that out, to know *if*, *when*, and *how* you should intervene to prevent calamities.

It might be easier if leaders like Jobs, Musk, and Holmes were normal people. But they're not. Steve Jobs called himself a misfit—the round peg in the square hole, someone who thinks differently.

He was right all the way around. Dominant visionaries do not act or think like most people. Each is a bundle of contradictions. They challenge convention at almost every turn, have the innate ability to create things others can't, and generate a bewildering swarm of opportunities and challenges in their wake. They are inherently complicated. On good days they are pioneers, trailblazers, and mavericks. On bad days they are troublemakers and rabble-rousers. Their strengths often cover up critical weaknesses and inexperience. And they can be extremely hard to manage—their unorthodox and domineering behavior stifles traditional governance approaches.

There has been and will always be a place for inspired geniuses who seek to do things in a radical new way. Thomas Edison and Edwin Land were visionaries who broke rules, challenged the status quo, and

reconfigured industries in the nineteenth and twentieth centuries.

Today we have a new set of ingenious leaders
attempting to construct better ways for us to live and
work. Betting on them makes sense. Steve Jobs, Marc
Benioff, and others have proved that a brilliant, inventive CEO can create a great company. That is the reason these mavericks are embraced by investors.

This book is about how to understand ingenious
leaders and what makes them go haywire. It describes
how to survive and thrive with them—and that's not as
easy as it sounds. Most people don't know how to work
with them to a successful outcome. Not only are these
leaders hard to work with, sometimes they're hard to
stomach. But unassisted and ungoverned, they won't
reach their full potential and, worse, can spin the company they built into a destructive orbit. They all need
help to make their vision a reality.

WHAT YOU WILL LEARN

We wrote *The Brilliant Jerk Conundrum* for the many
people affected by dominant visionaries: investors who
bet on the domineering leaders to create game-changing companies; senior management teams and
employees who have to collaborate with and guide the
far-seeing thinkers; the general public that wonders
what in the world is going on in these organizations;
and the company boards that have the responsibility
to govern.

The Brilliant Jerk Conundrum is a natural continuation of our first book, *Making Innovation Work.* That book covered almost every aspect of innovation, but one element continued to perplex us. As we surveyed the expanding innovation experience and knowledge base, we wondered how to best harness the creative talents of a wunderkind like Steve Jobs. He challenged the usual concepts of innovative leaders. We saw Jobs' initial vision and relentless drive take Apple to the forefront of companies around the world, and then he seemingly self-destructed—and left Apple in disarray. He returned, and his pioneering leadership propelled the company to unparalleled success.

What was different about Jobs' first and second episodes at Apple? This question presented a new set of issues: When is it advisable to challenge a quixotic leader like Jobs and when is it best to leave them alone to work their magic? How can you decide which action to take? What are the roles of the investors, venture capitalists (VCs), executives, and board? We knew these were important questions, but we did not have the answers.

Marc had worked on the postmortem of the Enron disaster (see page 53 for a description), so we were well aware of the havoc that came when a trailblazing founder was not challenged and mistakes compounded into a financial catastrophe. Enron proved there was a clear need for those tasked with governance to be able to sniff out a problem and prevent a disaster when a beguiling, relentless disrupter was in charge.

But that was only one part of the answer. Getting in the way of a talented but sometimes irrational leader who was on a mission to change the world could kill a once-in-a-lifetime opportunity to create wealth and indelibly influence consumer culture. We needed to know how to tell the difference between an ingenious CEO on track to create a groundbreaking innovation and one on a destructive path. Then there was the conundrum of what to do for each situation. So we lacked clear, complete answers, but at least we had defined the problem: *if, when,* and *how* to intervene with a dominant visionary.

We saw more brainiac leaders grabbing the headlines—some for feats of brilliance and others for boneheaded mistakes. They provided a bunch of real-life examples to fuel our research. As part of our exploration, Marc posed the questions of *if, when,* and *how* to intervene with a dominating ingenious CEO at a presentation to a group of governance professionals. The room lit up with energy. Their reaction confirmed this was a critical area of inquiry . . . and they wanted answers. That fueled our mission.

We reviewed our work with boards and some of those unruly, exceptional CEOs. We scoured articles and books written about visionaries to gather the collective wisdom and identify key issues. And, to get the inside story, we talked to scores of board members and others involved in managing a variety of dominant visionaries and brainy jerks. It became clear that this was an untapped, rich opportunity. No one had tackled this issue.

This book describes how to meet the challenges and opportunities created by dominant visionaries and how to generate and protect value when an authoritarian trailblazer is leading the charge. Our book uses the stories of seven leaders to depict the range of characteristics common to dominant visionaries. Two important lessons emerge. The first is that the presence of a revolutionary leader requires special handling; the traditional rules don't apply. With an inspired and highly controlling powerhouse at the helm, boards, investors, and employees need to be ready for a different kind of journey.

The second lesson is that the best actions to govern, thrive, and survive depend on the type of visionary you are dealing with. Not all dominant visionaries are the same. With some visionaries, there is a real risk of getting in the way and curtailing the value they could create. But with other types, complacency is a huge mistake. Left unsupervised, their behavior could destroy the company.

There are proven ways to work with the different types of dominant visionaries. Drawing on the hard-won lessons of board members, investors, and employees that have experienced a commanding innovator's escapades, we describe the best ways to protect and enhance value creation and create a safe, sane working environment.

Members of the board and executives were forthcoming about what worked and what didn't, but because what goes on in companies, and especially in boardrooms, is not public information, in many cases they required we keep confidential the names of companies and individuals.

We divided this book into two parts. The first defines the problem, and the second describes the solution.

Part One: Understanding the Conundrum goes beyond the headlines and news stories and provides a closer look at the whirlwind world a force-of-nature chief executive can create. We wanted to give you an inside look at what makes these amazing people tick. Chapter 1 describes what a dominant visionary is and why boards, investors, and employees are drawn to them. There is an attraction to an imaginative leader with an ingenious new model for success.

Focusing a company around a charismatic founder makes a lot of sense early on. Their disruptive vision creates a magnetic story that attracts investors, customers, and employees. But over the long run, the history of these eccentric, far-seeing leaders is mixed. There are risks that come with a brilliant founder who has strong control of company decisions but lacks sufficient check.

Some genius leaders soar and achieve great success. Others crash and burn. Why? We identify three phenomena that contribute to problems with domineering brainiacs: asymmetric power, where the authoritative genius has control of the board; a cult of personality that blinds people to what is really going on; and opaqueness, the lack of critical information, which keeps the board and others in the dark.

In chapter 2 we present snapshots of seven revolutionary leaders and their companies—Steve Jobs and Apple, Elon Musk and Tesla, Elizabeth Holmes and Theranos, Larry Page and Google, Travis Kalanick and Uber, Jeff Bezos and Amazon, and Ken Lay at Enron. We chose these short stories because they cover the range of visionaries—from winners who can be jerks to jerks who became losers. The snapshots exemplify the major challenges and opportunities inherent with unorthodox, spellbinding CEOs.

Chapter 3 describes the reasons for bad behavior among this type of leader. When we look across the spectrum of these extraordinary personalities, we see brilliance combined with stubbornness and a penchant for breaking rules—a recipe for a feast of misconduct. One of the most interesting aspects of these talented leaders is that they can shift behaviors over time. They may start out acting as role models but deteriorate into displaying unattractive behaviors. Some become massive jerks or liars—or both.

Most of the approaches for dealing with a forceful, groundbreaking CEO have not worked well. There have been too many catastrophes and near catastrophes in recent years to feel we have the problem under control. However, there are approaches that work.

Part Two: Solving the Puzzle describes the best ways for you to deal with a wunderkind in the top slot. Chapter 4 covers the challenge of governing one with traditional approaches. While standard board roles and responsibilities can handle some issues quite well, a radical or maverick poses special challenges, and corporate governance principles and processes need to shift.

We provide the key elements for you to solve the puzzle of working with a dominant visionary in chapter 5. The chapter illustrates how you can work with a genius chief executive, including *if, when* and *how* to intervene. Chapter 6 explains how you as stakeholders—VCs, executives, employees, or investors—can thrive and survive in the presence of a strong-willed powerhouse. We want to make it clear: the rules for survival change when you work in a company led by a dominant visionary. Whether you are an executive, employee, or investor, you need to change some behaviors.

While chapters 4, 5, and 6 get specific about how to overcome obstacles and govern effectively, chapter 7 distills the essence of the approach and offers a cautionary tale from an unlikely source of how not to handle a genius in the lead—a contentious performance of a Brahms concerto. It turns out iron-willed visionary leaders are not limited to the business world.

By the end of the book, you will have new insights into why we have brainy visionaries and why some of them produce great results while others turn into jerks or, in extreme cases, felons. And you will have a road map of how to productively work with and support the charismatic but often challenging leader, circumvent nasty situations, and steer a course to value creation in a robust company. If you work with or around a disrupter-in-chief—someone who lives to challenge norms and the status quo—we made this book for you.

PART ONE

UNDERSTANDING
THE CONUNDRUM

We built this book to answer several questions. The first was *Why do some visionary leaders create value while others generate havoc?* To understand, we talked to experienced board members, discussed the realities of high-energy ingenious leaders and the people around them, reviewed the popular and academic literature, and analyzed groundbreaking leaders who exemplify the range of ways a gifted impresario at the helm can sink or soar, along with the company.

It became clear, during the course of our work, that dominant visionaries are not like most people. They excel at many things but are not great at all things. Their strengths often cover up weaknesses or inexperience that hamper their pursuit to change the world. We explored what these unorthodox talents have accomplished—from brilliant successes to massive failures and everything in between—and developed an understanding of what makes them the way they are.

In this section, chapter 1 describes the factors that can lead to bad behaviors. Chapter 2 presents snapshots of the characteristics of seven ingenious leaders and their unique styles. To close out the conundrum discussion, in chapter 3 we describe the challenges of living with an imaginative CEO and governing their leadership.

CHAPTER 1

WITH A STRONG LEADER AT THE HELM, WHAT CAN POSSIBLY GO WRONG?

Investors, employees, and boards embrace governing geniuses when they want radical disruption or significant change—something robust and different to drive growth and transformation. This stance is a smart gamble. Clever, energetic visionaries are predisposed to take bold actions and drive change—they make a difference. When innovation and smart, aggressive risk-taking are called for, shrewd, hard-driving trailblazers are seen as the ones who can make things happen.

But it is a risk. When things go right, their wizardry can change industries and generate massive value for shareholders, employees, and society. Think Benioff at Salesforce and Jobs returning to Apple after his ouster by the board. Similarly, Reed Hastings' Netflix has made an indelible mark on the entire media industry. And Jeff Bezos' juggernaut, Amazon, has left competitors in its wake to become a convention-crushing bulldozer, the largest internet company by revenue, and the top retailer by market capitalization.

At the other end of the spectrum, dominant visionaries have created havoc. Striving to make their vision a reality, some earn the label of jerk, like Elon Musk, whose erratic behavior has caused indigestion for many investors and regulators.

Other business wizards, in their quest to change the status quo, have caused such damage that their companies disintegrated. Elizabeth Holmes and Ken Lay are tied for first place on the list of failed visionaries in that category. Enron was done in by CEO Ken Lay's off-balance-sheet financial shenanigans. Theranos' CEO, Elizabeth Holmes, lied about the company's so-called revolutionary blood-testing technology. The SEC fined her for defrauding investors of $700 million. Theranos, which once had a market capitalization of $9 billion, withered to nothing.

That is the inherent gamble with dominant visionaries. Some produce gargantuan wins; others implode the company.

TAXONOMY OF OUTCOMES

Why does this happen? Why do some unorthodox game changers create wealth while others destroy their companies? Part of the problem resides in the personality of a maverick who thrives on breaking rules and ignoring norms.

Creative wizards who assume the mantle of leadership often create an atmosphere of infallibility—best described as *executive omniscience*. They do things that make them look like superheroes and act like people for whom the normal rules don't apply. When this happens, the genius goes unchecked, becomes ungovernable, and can carry on in troublesome and destructive ways.

Three factors contribute to the illusion of executive omniscience.

- *Asymmetric power* where the chief executive has control of the board and can direct the outcome of any vote
- *Cult of personality* based on a magnetic, bigger-than-life personality that blinds people to what is really going on
- *Opaqueness* that blocks visibility into performance through control of information critical to decision-making and governance

Any one or two of these elements signals a potential problem. The presence of all three creates an environment ripe for abuse.

ASYMMETRIC POWER

Sometimes a majority of the control of the company is in the hands of a charismatic, high-energy CEO. That makes it hard, if not impossible, for investors or the board to make changes to leadership or control high-level decision-making.

Asymmetric control often is a result of dual class voting shares. This gives founders outsized voting rights through a special class of shares and insulates them from accountability.

Unequal voting rights were developed to keep corporate control in the hands of a founder or a founder's family. Dodge Brothers' initial public offering (IPO) in 1925, and Ford's IPO in 1956 are early examples of these dual class systems established to keep family control of the companies even as they welcomed public shareholders. Berkshire Hathaway puts control of the company firmly in the hands of Warren Buffett and has a second class of stock with limited voting rights.

This structured approach for board control came back into vogue with Google's dual class listing in 2004. They were followed by other tech companies including Facebook, Groupon, and LinkedIn. Alibaba, wishing to implement a dual class structure, chose to list on the New York Stock Exchange in 2014, because Hong Kong did not then permit dual class listings (the Hong Kong Exchange has since opened to dual class listings). Alibaba's governance structure includes a partnership that elects the majority of the board. Snap made dual share history by being the first company that issued nonvoting shares in its IPO. Dual class share listings in the US increased 44 percent over ten years—from 487 in 2005, to 701 in 2015.

Dual class shares are a *give-and-take* proposition. On the plus side, the structure *gives* founders control so they can resist undue shareholder pressure and pursue their vision. However, the dual class structure gives disproportionate control to the founders' shareholding and *takes* power from shareholders. The favored shareholders cannot be booted out even if they fail to produce brilliant results or their performance declines over the years. And the asymmetry makes it nearly impossible for shareholders or the board to change that structure. Investors and the board relinquish their governance rights in the belief that the founding entrepreneurs can produce huge value and the potential returns on the stock will outweigh governance concerns. That can be a dangerous bet.

Share structure is not the only way top-dog visionaries seize control. Dominance in the organization can be achieved through more traditional forms of control. Jeff Bezos does not have the voting shares to control the board, but he maintains a solid grip on the huge Amazon empire by dint of his brilliance and ability to repeatedly challenge and engage his leadership team. His company principles and structured team meetings make his direction clear and present on what must be done. While he cannot be everywhere, all Amazon employees know what Jeff would do if he were in their shoes.

Some forceful founders use their oversized personas and control of information to create an asymmetric power base. They know how to get people to go along with their ideas through personality and charisma. Steve Jobs' mind-set permeated the company because of his outsized personality and domineering management style. His operating mantra, to aggressively push for massive change, was invoked by staff even when he was not in the room. It was common to hear "What would Steve do?" in Apple meetings. With that phrase hanging in the room, people would set out to solve the problem as if Steve himself were in the room calling the shots.

CULT OF PERSONALITY

All good entrepreneurs are skilled at persuasion. They are natural salespeople. But dominant visionaries possess a special magnetism. They are great storytellers and amazingly adept at convincing others to join their quest to change the world. That creates a cult of personality.

Almost everyone has heard of Steve Jobs' uncanny ability to get people to do things they thought were impossible. Bud Tribble at Apple Computer coined the term *reality distortion field* in 1981 to describe Steve's mind-bending effect on the developers working on the Macintosh project. "In [Jobs'] presence, reality is malleable. He can convince anyone of practically anything," Tribble said. True: Steve used his magnetic personality and charisma to get people to join his quest and go along with his vision to "put a dent in the universe" via Apple's new technologies. But he did not limit this distortion field to his project teams. He used his personality force field every time he wanted to get people to go along with his way of doing things or to do things they didn't know they could. His teams were so committed they would walk through walls for him.

In the early days of Theranos, Elizabeth Holmes was compared to Steve Jobs. She dressed in black turtlenecks and compared Theranos' proprietary blood-testing technology to the iPod. Like Steve, she paid close attention to creating and delivering a strong company narrative emphasizing how different Theranos was and how it would change the world. She said, "There isn't a company that does what we do. We're creating a new space."

She used her well-developed persuasive powers to create a cult of personality around that vision. As a result, she developed an immensely strong following among her staff and investors. She had the same effect on her board of directors, including Henry Kissinger. "Elizabeth's iron determination and great intellectual ability turned me from a mild skeptic to an enthusiast," and she "has a sort of ethereal quality," Kissinger said. Speaking for the board, he said, "We aren't exactly a group of people who give away our time lightly." In hindsight, Kissinger's assessment of her brilliance and leadership potential was badly flawed—based more on her magnetic personality and charisma than on facts.

A cult of personality can not only mesmerize people into believing half truths and lies, it often produces a headstrong CEO so committed to getting their way that they resort to bullying and silencing differing viewpoints through intimidation or force. The resulting company culture is pockmarked with fear. Offering a contrary point of view or engaging in constructive criticism of the boss's approach is a recipe for failure. Theranos employees who raised a concern or an objection to Holmes' way of doing things were branded naysayers, a threat to the success of the company. Those who persisted were marginalized or fired.

Holmes is not the only one guilty of abuse. HealthTap founder Ron Gutman "committed acts of intimidation, abuse, and mistrust" and "repeatedly mistreated, threatened, harassed and verbally abused employees," according to his termination letter from the board. "This leaves us with no choice but to fire you," the letter reads. "The toxicity you introduced into the workplace ends now."

When an iron-willed firebrand operates under the assumption that they have the right to be demanding and abusive, some employees and partners are repelled and depart. Others, captivated by charisma, remain steadfast in their loyalty.

OPAQUENESS

Limited access to information keeps people in the dark and hides what is really going on in the company. Opaque environments are created in several ways.

Groupthink is one of the most common types of opaqueness. It creates blind spots that lead smart people to overlook obvious or impending challenges and make bad decisions. Irving Janis identified the problem and the ways to overcome groupthink way back in the 1970s. But groupthink is still with us and leads politicians into military misadventures and plays havoc with corporate boards. It has been blamed for the ill-judged invasion and occupation of Iraq and the Volkswagen emissions scandal.

Think about the years leading up to 2008 and how the banks maintained their course until they ran aground and the financial crisis ensued. Similarly, today we have data-think, where everyone relies on the same information at the same time guaranteeing everyone will be wrong about the same thing at the same time. That is the force that brought hedge fund Long-Term Capital Management and the entire financial system close to collapse in 1998.

The Enron board suffered from a self-inflicted blind spot when they did not dig deeply enough to understand the novel financial model employed by founder Ken Lay and CEO Jeffrey Skilling. Lay and Skilling assured the board that the off-balance-sheet engineering was working brilliantly. The Enron board included several financial and accounting heavy hitters, but apparently they never explored the off-balance-sheet approach. They kept their heads in the sand and never got a glimpse of the financial malfeasance going on. The blind spot kept them from seeing that Enron's financial model was a ticking time bomb.

Hypercontrol of information also creates opaqueness. Steve Jobs forbade Apple employees from communicating among themselves regarding what they were working on. Information flowed one direction at Apple—up. Only people at the top knew what was going on—and only in their area of operations. No one questioned the practice of withholding information. It was the mandated behavior and cultural norm inside Apple. As a result, Steve, who sat at the very top of the organization, had the most information and the best company-wide perspective. Coupled with his reality distortion field, he had the power to control and manage information and perspectives to his advantage.

Micromanagement, hypersecretiveness, and constrained sharing are not inherently wrong or evil intentioned. Apple has become one of the most successful companies in history and continues to tightly control information within the organization. But it can work out differently.

Elizabeth Holmes controlled the information, and all major decisions in Theranos went through her. She would not divulge to anyone how the Theranos technology worked—not even the board. She wrapped a cloak of secrecy around the proprietary technology. Holmes said Theranos would not discuss how its technology worked, invoking the need to protect the company's intellectual property and avoid tipping off potential competitors.

Instead of illuminating the source of Theranos' competitive advantage or describing how things were really going, she offered self-referential pronouncements that shaded the real situation. "Success is not the result of spontaneous combustion. You must set yourself on fire" is one of her most remembered and ridiculed statements about how Theranos was going to change the world. Her tight control of information hid the fact that Theranos' technology was not performing as claimed until a pesky journalist dug deep, uncovered the fraud, and blew the whistle. Then the Theranos house of cards came tumbling down.

CONTRIBUTORS TO THE ILLUSION OF EXECUTIVE OMNISCIENCE

Asymmetric power

Cult of personality

Opaqueness

Not all companies with enigmatic, charismatic trailblazers succumb to the illusion of executive omniscience. Many have some of the three elements and still perform admirably. That's one reason it is hard for executives, investors, and boards to know what to do.

UNDERSTANDING YOUR NONCONFORMIST CEO

Most of the stories we hear about business visionaries deal with founders like Steve Jobs and Jeff Bezos who build new companies and define a new industry or redefine the competitive dynamics of an existing one. But visionaries are also used to transform established enterprises. When an old-dog company needs to learn new tricks, usually after a decline in growth and the erosion of a leadership position, boards often bet on savvy visionaries to bring new verve to the company.

HP's board tapped Meg Whitman to lead a transformation in Silicon Valley's original garage start-up success story. When competitive dynamics and new technologies threatened, GE's board tapped Jeff Immelt to transition the company. And IBM brought up Ginni Rometty to orchestrate the company to meet new competitive dynamics.

These corporate change agents may not sound like the firebrands you typically see in start-up founders. And they're not, because these leaders must bring about transformation in established enterprises without being crushed by the organizational antibodies that fight change. They were embraced by their board, investors, and employees because they were seen as trailblazers who could bring innovation, transformation, and savvy risk-taking—the same call to action as start-up founders.

Board challenges related to asymmetric power, a cult of personality, and opaqueness occur in companies of all sizes. We recently worked with a family-owned company that had a market cap approaching $1 billion.

At the age of seventy-five, the founder and CEO was struggling with major control and succession issues. He wanted to soon turn over control to his children. But his dominant leadership and complete control of the board had him stymied.

The board consisted of three independent members along with the founder and his four adult children. The children had not been involved with the business, lacked real business training, and voted as directed by their father. The other board members were technically independent, in that they were not employees or family. But they were longtime friends of the founder and also voted as told.

To move forward, the board needed to redistribute the balance of power. With our guidance, the board became stronger. We counseled the board to reduce the chief executive's control and interference. The adult children needed to vote based on genuine understanding of the issues. The company established a process that enhanced their business acumen. First, the board educated the children on the issues coming before the board prior to each meeting. The board also established a training program to empower them to more actively participate in the company and therefore prepare for an eventual company transition.

We counseled that privately held and family-controlled companies can benefit—significantly—from having independent directors, if they act independently. Otherwise their participation is just window dressing.

Though they do not have voting control, independent directors provide impartial and contrary opinions.

Our story of this client engagement is not just a study of a family-run business. It exemplifies what happens when a strong, dominant leader builds a successful company but puts it at risk through restrictive, confounding management practices. We have seen this play out countless times in companies of all sizes and with different types of CEOs. Our advice: unless the chief executive receives more independent and business-savvy advice and begins building a transition path for his successors, the company's long-term future is bleak. That scenario is part of the formula for success in all companies with an authoritarian boss.

It would be a grave mistake to assume dominant visionaries and hard-driving revolutionaries are someone else's concern. Don't assume they only show up in someone else's C-suite. They can show up anywhere—including the top, middle, or bottom of your organization. Or in a supply-chain partner you have to deal with. You need to be ready because, almost without exception, they make life difficult for everyone around them—employees, investors, suppliers, regulators, and board members.

The following chapters describe ways you can thrive despite difficulty, tolerate the uncertainty, and manage the best and the worst a commanding and imaginative leader brings. The next chapter presents stories that show how difficult it is to join forces with and govern these domineering CEOs.

CHAPTER 2

SNAPSHOTS OF HUBRIS

People usually put stories about dominant visionaries in two buckets: winners and losers. Winners disrupt industries and generate incredible value. Losers implode and destroy value. But being a winner or loser is not always that clear-cut or permanent. A dominant visionary can be a saint *and* a sinner—first a brash winner and then a wounded loser. Or vice versa.

Some losers are reborn as winners. Steve Jobs' return from exile in 1997 to lead Apple is remarkable in that regard. Or sometimes, winners go astray and slide ignominiously into the loser category. Originally, Travis Kalanick at Uber was hailed as a superhero of business-model disruption. Not long after, Kalanick was forced out by the board for conduct unbecoming a leader. After his exit, most industry watchers have dumped him in the loser bucket and act as if he has no future. But who knows? His next leadership role might put him back in the winner category.

We know trailblazers can see farther and better than most people. They envisage entirely new ways of doing things—whether it's using a computer to find the best place to eat or arranging a ride to the selected restaurant. But it goes even further than the power of foresight. One veteran board member said, "They also have the ability to see around corners." Maybe, but in addition to seeing better, they have the uncanny ability to veer off course.

This chapter contains snapshots of seven leading visionaries. Some are winners, some are losers, and the jury is still out on others. This is a relatively small number of stories given the large number of examples we have seen and studied. The small number chosen here is inversely proportional to their importance. All seven are gems—excellent examples of the wide range of what can happen when a disrupter takes charge. They highlight the governance challenges and prominent elements of the forces that shape the outcome with hard-charging visionaries—asymmetric power, cult of personality, and opaqueness.

ASYMMETRIC POWER

Many iron-willed visionaries have a lock on control of the company. Some tip control of the board to their favor via a dual share structure. Some use powers of persuasion and information control to get their way. While it gives founders more latitude to pursue their vision, asymmetry can undermine the ability to challenge bad decisions and rein in bad behaviors and counterproductive actions.

TRAVIS KALANICK AND UBER

Right from the start, Uber's business was based on breaking rules and attempting to establish an unfair advantage. CEO Travis Kalanick's new business model mounted a headlong attack on the taxi business—a tightly regulated business in most cities. Instead of negotiating or persuading regulators to give Uber room to operate, Kalanick ignored the regulations and elbowed his way into markets. "We're in a political campaign," Kalanick said, "and the candidate is Uber and the opponent is an asshole named Taxi." Kalanick's highly combative sensibilities permeated Uber's operating model and culture. Every challenge was seen as an opportunity to demonstrate Uber's aggressive will to dominate and win.

After the 2010 Uber launch in San Francisco, Kalanick expanded quickly. First in the US—including Seattle, New York, Boston, Chicago—and then to foreign cities. While the response from users was often positive, others hated Uber. There were street riots by taxi drivers in London, Paris, Berlin, and other European cities. Regulators were infuriated and up in arms; Uber was fined and banned in cities around the world. In Seoul, Kalanick was indicted in absentia. France arrested Uber executives.

The confrontation did not deter growth. By 2014, less than four years after launch, Kalanick had established Uber in over 250 cities and over 50 countries, and Kalanick's disruptive business model and Uber's stellar growth rate attracted high-profile investors. Josh Kopelman of First Round, who provided the initial seed capital, said, "What we really look for is that contrarian idea, the idea where the founder thinks they have a view of the world that other people laugh at." Many savvy investors seek that kind of disrupter. Their brashness and bravado are funding magnets that attract early-stage financing in the hopes of a very big win.

Benchmark Capital jumped in later, taking a 20 percent stake in 2010. Later rounds included big-name funds such as Summit Partners, Kleiner Perkins, Menlo Ventures, and Texas Pacific Group. Technology companies got in on the action too—Google, Alibaba, and Microsoft invested, as well as prominent individuals such as Jeff Bezos. Uber's 2016 fund-raising round gave the company a valuation of $68 billion, making it the largest pre-IPO company in the US. In 2019, just prior to the IPO, Uber's valuation was reported to be estimated as high as $100 billion to $120 billion. The company priced the offered shares at $45, giving it a value of approximately $82 billion.

Kalanick drove Uber's hypergrowth by breaking rules and crashing conventions. He adopted an equally aggressive strategy regarding the terms of investment. Kalanick and his cofounders designed a system to retain control through a dual class share structure. The structure gave them a controlling vote on board matters and the ability to name most members of the board of directors. Investing in Uber was heralded as a bet that Kalanick could disrupt the status quo and supplant it with a new model. But Kalanick's dual class share structure and organizational control of the board made investing in Uber a vote in support of his unconstrained power to lead the company. At the time, he was the epitome of a VC's dream of a great bet.

Everywhere the company went, it transformed city transportation with Kalanick's new business model. But challenges kept mounting, and some of the luster came off the original premise. Uber drivers launched a class-action suit against Uber, arguing they should be classified as employees rather than contractors—a major challenge to Uber's financial model. Crimes committed by Uber drivers raised concerns about the Uber business model of arms-length contracting of drivers. The discontent bubbled up in social media, and public opinion against the company rocketed to new heights. But despite the increasing problems, the Uber board did not blink. They maintained support for Kalanick even though two hundred thousand people wiped the Uber app from their phones. Lyft, Uber's major competitor, gained significant market share amid the turmoil.

To add to the misery, Susan Fowler, a former Uber engineer, posted a damning blog alleging a pattern of sexual harassment that went unchecked by Uber's HR department and senior management. At this point, with the company entering what looked like a death spiral, the board swung into action. Eric Holder, former US attorney general, was hired to lead an investigation into Uber's culture. Another board-sponsored inquiry took on the challenge of investigating Fowler's accusations and other claims of misconduct that were piling up.

While the sexual harassment and cultural investigations were ongoing, Waymo, the self-driving division established by Google, filed a lawsuit alleging Uber knowingly colluded to steal proprietary Waymo information. If true, the charge would threaten Uber's reputation and financial stability.

As things worsened, the situation became precarious; Kalanick's rule-breaking approach seemed out of control. But he dominated the board and its decisions and stayed at the helm. Just when it looked as if nothing else could possibly go wrong, a video of Kalanick verbally attacking an Uber driver spread across social media. With a public-relations storm swirling around Kalanick, board member Arianna Huffington proposed an addition to Uber's list of cultural values: *No brilliant jerks allowed.* Undeterred, Kalanick remained chief executive and retained control of the company.

The board's investigations painted a nasty picture of Kalanick's leadership and its effects on Uber's culture. A compliance officer said, "If you changed some of the business and legal language, you might well think you were reading a report on *Animal House.*"

The board-sponsored reports called for sweeping changes in Uber's culture and management. The severity of the situation was not lost on Uber's board. They voted unanimously to adopt the report's recommendations. The report relating to discrimination, sexual harassment, unprofessional behavior, and bullying drilled into 215 staff complaints. It recommended that Uber take disciplinary action in over fifty cases: management took action, and more than twenty employees were fired.

The board announced that Kalanick would take a leave of absence, during which time his responsibilities would be shared among a group of fourteen direct reports. But, unwilling to cede control and effectively raising a middle finger to the board, Kalanick continued to leverage his asymmetrical voting power and even attempted to add new board seats to bolster his dominant position.

Benchmark, which still held a seat on the board, took the unprecedented step of suing Kalanick, citing "gross mismanagement and other misconduct at Uber," including Uber's intellectual property violations against Waymo and sexual harassment allegations. Benchmark accused Kalanick of breach of fiduciary duty and requested his removal from the board. Unsurprisingly, Kalanick vowed to fight the lawsuit. He refused to relinquish the power he had been given when he took the reins of the company.

During this turmoil, in August 2017, Uber announced that Dara Khosrowshahi, CEO of Expedia, would replace Kalanick as chief executive officer and assume one of the vacant board seats. Upon accepting the job, Khosrowshahi said, "This company has to change. What got us here is not what's going to get us to the next level." Kalanick's reign was over.

Travis Kalanick's penchant for breaking rules was the thing that made Uber an early success. He opened new income opportunities for thousands and challenged regulations by starting Uber in violation of restrictive rules regarding transportation licensing. In the process, Kalanick alienated huge swaths of the public and many of Uber's drivers. He also created a company culture where law breaking and sexual harassment were allowed. His control of the board made him immune to any criticism and left his bad-boy destructive behaviors unchecked. It almost sank the company.

LARRY PAGE AND GOOGLE

To sustain early-stage growth, Google founders Larry Page and Sergey Brin—two twentysomething graduate student computer nerds from Stanford—explored a capital injection from the Silicon Valley venture capital community. Page had a nonnegotiable requirement for investors: Page and Brin would retain a majority of the voting stock and maintain control of Google. Some VCs balked at Page's thumb on the scales of board control. VCs typically wanted board power more evenly distributed, so they had a say in how the company was run.

Eventually, Kleiner Perkins and Sequoia Capital agreed with Page's terms and invested $25 million. But they had their own requirement: in exchange for Page and Brin maintaining majority ownership, they wanted Page to step down as CEO. They said they wanted a world-class, experienced chief executive to help build a top-flight management team.

Both sides agreed to the terms and the deal closed. It was reported that months later, Page called John Doerr, the lead partner from Kleiner Perkins, and said he had second thoughts about stepping down. Page said he and Brin could run the company themselves; no external CEO was needed.

Doerr was uncomfortable with Page staying in the leadership position. Page did not have experience running a company and would not be able to navigate the inherent challenges of growing the start-up and attaining scale. He enticed Page to meet with several highly respected tech chief executives, including Apple's Steve Jobs, Bezos at Amazon, and Andy Grove at Intel. Page came away from the conversations convinced Google could use a savvy, experienced boss at the helm. Page and Doerr scouted the tech community. Eric Schmidt, chief executive of Novell, emerged as the best choice. He had great experience in tech and a solid reputation as a leader, and he had actually done coding early in his career—something Page, who was still close to his coding roots, considered a big plus. And Schmidt was a Burner—one of the many, including Page, who attended the annual Burning Man festival. The Google board hired Schmidt as chairman in March 2001; he became CEO in August of that year.

Schmidt acted as the adult in the room—the senior executive with a seasoned perspective and solid operating experience. He balanced the excellent vision and drive of Page and Brin with proven, sharp operating capabilities that were essential for scaling and growth.

This type of adult supervision was not new in Silicon Valley. Outsider CEOs had proven to be valuable in the past: Jim Barksdale at Netscape Communications, Meg Whitman at eBay Inc., and Carol Bartz at Autodesk all had successful track records in Silicon Valley.

Googlers honored Schmidt's leadership. He ran the management meetings, controlled the agenda, and mediated key senior level interactions. His responsibilities included "building the corporate infrastructure needed to maintain Google's rapid growth as a company," according to Google. But many still considered founder Page the boss. Page stayed engaged in debate and decisions on key issues. He approved every hire and kept a tight control on product development.

In 2007, many felt Page retreated a bit from day-to-day operations. He insulated himself from meetings and restricted access to his calendar. It is reported that he even went so far as to get rid of his assistants to thwart executives arranging meetings through that back channel. But Page did not disappear. He continued as the behind-the-scenes helmsman as Google grew rapidly via internal growth and acquisitions. By 2010, Google had twenty-four thousand employees and a $180 billion capitalization.

Schmidt held the top executive position until 2011. At that point Page, Brin, and Schmidt agreed the time had come to make another major leadership change. In January 2011, Schmidt announced he was stepping down as CEO. Page was to assume that role going forward. Schmidt tweeted, "Day-to-day adult supervision no longer needed."

Page lost no time reasserting himself. He saw to it that existing products were improved, new products launched, and aggressive development of radical projects undertaken. He also made bold acquisitions of leading-edge companies. Under Page's leadership, Google continued to grow and prosper in line with his vision.

Then, Page set about making changes to the culture and operating style. In 2013, Page told his team that Google would have to cease internal fighting to secure its role as a creator of whole new markets and an unparalleled solution provider for wicked problems. The new rule was "zero tolerance for fighting." That edict shocked his team. In the early days of Google, Page was often the poster child for aggressive behavior and encouraged staff and leadership to adopt a combative style. Social niceties were discarded; confrontation was the norm. He saw rigorous inquiry—no matter how confrontational—as the acceptable cost of finding great solutions and making the right decisions.

But that was then. Page said the challenges Google faced were different now. To reach their full potential and thrive as a company, Google executives would need to learn to work together. Going forward, they needed to drop the combative spirit that had infused the earlier culture and work ethic. Collaboration was Google's new cultural imperative.

Then in 2016, Page, using his founder's mind-set and board power, made another major shift in Google's trajectory: Alphabet was born—a holding company that broke apart the bevy of companies that had grown up under the Google banner and created discernable business units. Page asserted the new structure would reenergize and focus the company—to get "more ambitious things done." Page stepped into the background and handed the chief executive role to Sundar Pichai.

In 2014, Google employee Andy Rubin was awarded a $150 million stock grant, an unusually large amount even by Google standards. The stock grant was to recognize Rubin's large contribution to Google's Android platform. It is not clear if Page or the board knew he was under investigation by the company for sexual harassment at that time. Google ultimately determined the charges were credible, but Rubin contested that judgment. Rubin eventually left the company with a $90 million severance agreement. Filing a lawsuit, investors claimed the board and executives failed in their governance responsibilities by allowing the big payout, keeping the whole thing quiet, and not curtailing the culture of sexual harassment that Rubin exemplified. The suit demonstrates the challenges arising when a strong, controlling founder takes actions that in hindsight the board should have had a bigger say in.

Page set the initial direction and culture of Google. When Schmidt stepped in as CEO, Page took a lower profile but ensured the initial vision was maintained. When Schmidt exited the CEO position, Page exerted a founder's prerogative with full control of the board. He altered the company's culture and structure to better enable his unchanged vision: *To build products that leverage technology to solve huge problems for millions of people.*

Page's control of the board has not led to the fiasco we saw with Kalanick at Uber. The addition of adult supervision provided a voice of experience to the management team, avoiding many potential missteps and contentious issues. However, now the perspective of a seasoned adviser is gone, and there are new challenges ahead for Google as tech companies come under increased scrutiny. Page's asymmetric board power may yet become a factor as Google maneuvers through the trials ahead.

CULT OF PERSONALITY

Some founders develop cult status. They craft an operating style and distinctive personal brand that can include disregarding or breaking rules and social norms—being the bad boy or girl with a vision to change the world. Mark Zuckerberg emerged as the kid wizard of social interaction who challenges traditional bounds of information sharing. Peter Thiel holds forth as the contrarian utopian with diabolically clever insights.

Using personality to create an extremely strong following among staff, investors, and the board creates room for the visionary to build their dream. But it can cloud perceptions of right and wrong and dissolve rational business discussions into the overly simple question of being either for me or against me.

ELON MUSK AND TESLA

To those who are believers, Elon Musk, CEO of Tesla, looks like David battling the Goliaths of industry. Tesla's electric vehicles have already upended the traditional automobile leaders. As Musk has pushed into the auto market, major manufacturers around the world have pivoted to meet his challenge and embrace electric vehicles.

Elon Musk did not start Tesla. He invested $6.6 million in 2004 and became the company's chairman. Not long after he became CEO, Musk stated that the goals of his entrepreneurial portfolio revolved around his vision to change the world and humanity. "The overarching purpose of Tesla Motors (and the reason I am funding the company) is to help expedite the move from a mine-and-burn hydrocarbon economy toward a solar electric economy," Musk wrote in a 2006 document he called "The Secret Tesla Motors Master Plan." Tesla and SolarCity were Musk's vehicles to reduce global warming through sustainable energy production and consumption.

Musk is active on many fronts. He is using batteries to plug the longstanding energy-storage hole in the electric power industry. His SpaceX venture aims to reduce the "risk of human extinction" by establishing a colony on Mars. The Boring Company tunneling technology could be a transportation game changer.

Musk casts an extremely big shadow. He epitomizes the reason so many people place their total trust in a leader with a view on changing the world. He has a heady vision and does not shy away from challenges. Instead he seems to run straight at them. "We're making a bet on Elon Musk," said one top-twenty Tesla investor. He compared Musk to Steve Jobs, saying, "These people are geniuses. You either believe in him or you don't."

Not everyone has bought into the Musk bravado. To nonbelievers, Musk's visions seem untethered to reality. Those folks are convinced he is going to lose his gamble to bring the technologies to commercial reality.

Musk doubters have placed their bets accordingly. Tesla was the most shorted stock in the world in 2018, in part because the short sellers believed Musk would burn through all the available cash and not reach positive cash flow working on Tesla's Model 3 production glitches. Nonbelievers have seen other firebrands fail to upend the auto giants like GM, Daimler, and Nissan. They bet Musk will end up another bold, brilliant failure. So far, Musk has proved them wrong.

Musk regularly stirs up his fan base by underscoring his self-confidence and willingness to rumble with the naysayers. He once bragged Tesla would be worth more than Apple someday, a statement that says more about his swagger than the realities of market capitalization. To tweak the multitude of stock short sellers, Musk sent an April Fools' tweet about the company going bankrupt. According to one Tesla investor, Musk says success only comes when there are people betting against you.

To reinforce his reputation as the brash bad-boy inventor, Musk conducts outlandish stunts. He sent a red Tesla sports car into orbit on one of his rockets with a space-suited dummy in the driver's seat. Why? Apparently, just because he could. And because his twenty-two million Twitter fans eat that sort of thing up.

Occasionally Musk gets testy. In May 2018, with Tesla's Model 3 production limping along, the company was bleeding cash at about $4 billion per year, more than $8,000 a minute, due to Model 3 manufacturing, which had been plagued by production snafus. Investors were worried. His retort: "Don't make a federal case out of it." Further questions at the investors meeting elicited a similar dismissal: "Boring, bonehead questions are not cool. Next?" Musk eventually apologized for his behavior saying it was foolish to ignore analysts. But, qualifying his apology, he added he still thought the questions were "bonehead" and "absurd."

Not long after the "bonehead episode," he turned on his charm to navigate his way through a challenging stockholder meeting. To mitigate concerns that he was becoming a total jerk, he addressed many of the same questions he had dismissed in the analyst meeting. Musk assured investors that Tesla would be cash-flow positive before the year's end. He had added a third shift at the company's San Francisco plant and approved expensive remedial actions to overcome the Model 3 manufacturing bottlenecks—including building an entirely new assembly line alongside the existing production facility. He won the day and survived stockholder challenges to his leadership and compensation.

Musk has rallied his fan base with talk of conspiracy. "As you know, there are a long list of organizations that want Tesla to die. These include Wall Street short sellers, who have already lost billions of dollars and stand to lose a lot more. Then there are the oil & gas companies, the wealthiest industry in the world—they don't love the idea of Tesla advancing the progress of solar power & electric cars. Don't want to blow your mind, but rumor has it that those companies are sometimes not super nice. Then there are the multitude of big gas/diesel car company competitors. If they're willing to cheat so much about emissions, maybe they're willing to cheat in other ways?" That sort of statement rallies his base of support but leaves nonbelievers scratching their heads.

At times, sobriety creeps into Musk's public statements. He said Tesla would never achieve its mission of accelerating "the world's transition to sustainable, clean energy" unless it proves it can become "sustainably profitable." Musk added an important observation: "That is a valid and fair criticism of Tesla's history to date." Musk's recognition of the importance of sustained profitability was a new, and to many, welcome addition to his business vision.

In 2018, Musk fired off a series of tweets about taking the company private. The SEC filed a lawsuit alleging Musk misled investors. Musk backed off the idea and reached a settlement with the SEC that allows him to remain CEO but requires he step aside from the chairman role for three years. Robyn Denholm, a veteran finance executive who joined Tesla's board four years ago became chairwoman. The settlement also required the addition of new independent board members. The board named a pair of new independent directors: Oracle chairman and tech-industry luminary Larry Ellison, and Kathleen Wilson-Thompson, the global head of human resources for Walgreens Boots Alliance. It is not clear what changes the new board members will bring. Larry Ellison had already expressed strong support for Musk before stepping onto the board. "I'm very close friends with Elon Musk, and I'm a big investor in Tesla."

Tesla's board has signaled it will step up the challenges of governing Musk. In a 2019 SEC filing (requiring shareholder approval), the board proposed reducing its size from eleven to seven members. The company described the shift as "increasing the proportion of newer directors with outside viewpoints to complement directors with a longstanding familiarity." Time will tell if the streamlined board is up to the task.

Elon Musk is the archetype of the brainy jerk. He has successfully brought massively ingenious technologies to commercial readiness. He rivals Thomas Edison in his ability to make things that people have only dreamed about. But periodically he seems to go berserk and leave people wondering what in the world is going on with him. Has he completely lost it, or is this bad-boy behavior just part of who he is? For employees and investors, the pressing question becomes, *is it time to jump ship?* There is a long list of his senior executives that have bailed out. And the board is faced with a key governance issue: *Is it time to try and rein him in, or should we just let him go and see what happens?*

Musk will continue to blaze a path forward. We can bet on him being occasionally obstreperous, and he will probably continue to relish taunting naysayers and sticking his finger in the eyes of those challenging him. For everyone besides Musk, and for stakeholders who are invested in the company's longevity, the question will be, What's the right thing to do about it?

JEFF BEZOS AND AMAZON

Jeff Bezos is a very tough and demanding boss. The Amazon culture he created is not for everyone. The rigors of the working environment—including long hours, hard-edged performance reviews, and a notoriously confrontational culture—were reported in the *New York Times* in 2015. While some find Amazon's environment uncomfortable, a large, dedicated following sees Bezos as an inspirational leader with the innovative force to change multiple industries. "We never claim that our approach is the right one—just that it's ours—and over the last two decades, we've collected a large group of like-minded people. Folks who find our approach energizing and meaningful," he wrote.

The fourteen leadership principles on the Amazon website and adhered to throughout the company, known internally as *Jeffisms*, are pure Bezos. They encapsulate the beliefs and operating style that make Bezos both loved and feared.

One of Bezos' most important principles makes it clear that adhering to established paths is not his style. "As we do new things, we accept that we may be misunderstood for long periods of time." Marching to a different drummer is part of the Bezos ethic— something to be proud of even if it confuses others.

Having a strong backbone is a must. "Do not compromise for the sake of social cohesion," the manifesto says. Employees should "respectfully challenge decisions when they disagree, even when doing so is uncomfortable or exhausting." Bezos is willing to challenge anyone and everyone in the spirit of improving the business.

"Be right, a lot," is another Jeffism. Failure happens, but it is not lauded as a virtue. Bezos and his leaders are expected to pick the winning solution more often than not. But they better not get too uppity. "Leaders do not believe their or their team's body odor smells of perfume," states another principle. For Bezos, results should be spectacular and speak for themselves.

Serving customers brilliantly and better than any other company is at the heart of the Amazon culture. Bezos is evangelical in his commitment to customer satisfaction—to look "around corners for ways to serve customers." A dissatisfied customer can contact Bezos directly via email. Bezos forwards the email to the person in Amazon responsible for addressing the issue. He adds only one thing—a question mark. The recipient of the *escalation*, as it's called at Amazon, works to resolve the issue in a few hours—faster is definitely better. Escalations are Bezos' way of making sure everyone knows he thinks customer satisfaction is always the top priority.

Bezos does not sit still. He is constantly exploring new opportunities to topple established players in other industries. Under Bezos' leadership, Amazon has created original streaming entertainment programs, becoming the first streaming company to win an Oscar for Best Picture. Amazon has launched into all aspects of retail, including food, and has become the leading cloud computing company. No business is safe from Bezos. His understated declaration of war is "Your margins are my opportunity."

Bezos has created a large dedicated following among many employees, investors, and his board. He combines his principles with a fierce, competitive mind-set and incorporates a take-no-prisoners business approach. By those that applaud his style, Bezos is seen as someone who can change the world. His board, investors, and followers are strong supporters of that vision.

Bezos does not have voting control of the Amazon board. He controls via energetic implementation of his vision, his magnetic personality, and a company culture defined by clear principles. The motto of his space company, Blue Origin, sums up his approach: *Gradatim Ferociter,* Latin for "step by step, ferociously." Some find the working environment too demanding. But many admire Jeff Bezos as an inspired change artist whose demands for excellence make success possible.

STEVE JOBS AND APPLE

Steve Jobs was many things. He was a visionary who reshaped entire industries. He was a genius at not only giving consumers what they wanted but sometimes giving them things they didn't know they wanted. His reality distortion field bent people to his ideas of what was possible. And he stormed onto the scene in Silicon Valley to "put a dent in the universe."

Jobs was also *not* some things you might expect. He "was not the world's greatest manager," Walter Isaacson, Steve's biographer, said. "In fact, he could have been one of the world's worst managers." Jobs had a flamethrower style. He was not always a nice guy. Sometimes he was a first-class asshole.

Walter Isaacson labeled Jobs' management style *Good Steve* and *Bad Steve.* Good Steve captured people's imaginations and turned a small computer company into gold. Bad Steve defined terrible behavior—he was petulant, publicly humiliated employees, and had a flair for unnecessary harshness and obscene rudeness.

Apparently, Jobs believed it was okay to be a jerk. Isaacson, who got to know Jobs well, said that "when he's very frustrated, his way to achieve catharsis is to hurt somebody. And I think he feels he has a liberty and license to do that. The normal rules of social engagement, he feels, don't apply to him."

"Even people who worked with Jobs told me that they'd seen him make people cry many times, but that 80 percent of the time he was right," said Bob Sutton, leadership professor at Stanford and author of the book *The No Assholes Rule*. Counseling Steve to offer constructive advice and avoid the personal attacks didn't change his behavior.

Good Steve and Bad Steve are only part of the story. His role as a force of nature was split into Jobs 1.0, the initial founding of Apple, and Jobs 2.0, his return from exile.

Jobs 1.0

Steve Jobs arose as a new, fresh force in business as the mercurial leader of Apple Computer. Jobs saw and said things differently than anyone else in tech.

The pace of Apple's early growth was stunning, largely built on his vision and two things he controlled very carefully: shipping computers with innovative graphical interfaces that delighted users ("Real artists ship" was one of his maxims) and establishing a highly differentiated brand that delivered a product that changed the way people used technology. Investors responded enthusiastically. The public offering on

December 12, 1980, sold out in minutes, raising $90 million—one of the most successful IPOs in history. Jobs was a hero—a new model for daring, inspired leadership. He had the support of the board and investors and was the darling of the business world—at least for a while.

Jobs and Steve Wozniak founded Apple Computer in 1976. Wozniak played the part of a highly gifted techie who saw the future in personal computers. He could make neat, new things. He complemented Jobs, who held center stage as the man with a vision, a storyteller par excellence, and someone with the grit to make big things happen.

Most people don't know that one of the elements that made Jobs successful was Mike Markkula. Without Markkula there would be no Apple, no Jobs. Markkula was the original investor in Apple because he saw the potential in the vision of Wozniak and Jobs. Jobs, Wozniak, and Markkula each had 26 percent of the stock, which meant any two could vote the other out. Markkula wrote the original business plan for Apple, took on the role of president in the early days, and helped Jobs grow into his leadership role. Jobs said Markkula was "like a father."

Markkula acted as a controlling force on some of Jobs' errant behavior. It was reported that Jobs, who had never been on a company board, removed his shoes during an Apple board meeting. "You're excused until you can behave like a board member," scolded Markkula. Jobs immediately put back on his shoes.

In 1983, with the company on an upward swing, Markkula prepared to step down as president. He said, "I didn't dislike being president and I did, I think, a damn good job." Markkula valued time with his wife and wanted to have time to pursue other interests. He was ready to step down as soon as Apple found somebody better. The company searched for replacements in the tech community—at IBM, DEC, HP, and Data General—but the fit of the candidates was not right. Apple broadened the search beyond tech companies and landed on John Sculley, head of PepsiCo. Hiring Sculley, a world-class marketer, made some sense. Apple had great technology but had to convince people who were unfamiliar with tech to use computers before they would make a purchase.

Sculley stepped into the management roles Markkula had designed and occupied. As president, Sculley reported to Jobs, the board chair. But Jobs, as head of the Macintosh group, reported to Sculley. That arrangement was highly unusual, but it had worked well for Jobs and Markkula. The arrangement put Jobs and Markkula in balanced proximity. Jobs could be the leader, and Markkula was able to influence Jobs on big and small issues. However, it turned into a big problem for Jobs and Sculley.

As the company struggled to compete against entrenched industry leaders, Jobs and Sculley became increasingly adversarial. Without the moderating influence of Markkula, Jobs became obstreperous and counterproductive. He felt besieged, and his leadership deteriorated.

The board backed Scully and took decisive action by firing Steve Jobs as chairman in 1985. Scully said that "in hindsight it probably would have been better to make Steve the CEO and I could have been the COO and chairman."

Jobs left Apple in a huff. His pride was wounded but his drive to make a difference was undaunted. He founded NeXT and enticed loyal software engineers from Apple to join him.

Jobs 2.0

Emerging from his highly visible exile, Jobs returned as part of Apple's purchase of NeXT in 1997. He shifted the company into a hyperproductive innovation engine unlike anything anyone had seen before. Apple launched the iPod, iPhone, and App Store. Growth was astronomical, and Jobs became a business legend.

Jobs 2.0 was a more seasoned executive, but he still had the dynamic of Good Steve, Bad Steve. He could charm you one moment and then turn on you later and chew you out ferociously in public. This marred his image, but with his vision and passion to change the world, he commanded extreme loyalty and support among employees, investors, and the board.

But his good luck ran out. Mid-2011, Steve Jobs resigned his position as chief executive officer of Apple and handed over leadership to Tim Cook. Jobs lost his long battle with pancreatic cancer on October 5, 2011.

Steve Jobs created a business juggernaut that dominated markets with remarkable products and brand. His vision and dynamic personality gave him one of the strongest followings in business. He accomplished in his second term at Apple what he could not in his first and secured his place as one of the greatest dominant visionaries of all time.

OPAQUENESS

When the boss controls the information and only doles out well-scrubbed pieces, the limited degree of access stifles constructive dissent and the review of options. This tight rein can also hide bad behaviors or worse, illegal activities.

Some hard-driving wunderkind manage information so tightly that investors, employees, and even the board do not see problems until it is too late. Ken Lay and Elizabeth Holmes are two examples of the huge negative consequences when a company's information is opaque.

KEN LAY AT ENRON

Northern Natural Gas Company formed in 1930 and became InterNorth through reorganizations and mergers—a major player in natural gas production and transmission. Houston Natural Gas, formed in 1925, was another large gas transmission company in the low-tech gas pipeline business. In 1984, Kenneth Lay, regarded widely as a pioneer and charismatic maverick, merged the two and changed the company's name to Enron.

Lay brought in Jeffrey Skilling from McKinsey as CEO, and the two set out to grow the company and modernize the industry. Rather than producing energy like a traditional energy company, Enron began trading energy and making a small margin on all trades. Acquiring Portland General Electric expanded its wholesale energy business and further diversified the company's activities. And as a trading firm that looked nothing like its old energy company beginnings, by 2000 the company was trading in broadband and fiber-optic networks.

Enron, lauded as the most innovative company in America by *Fortune* magazine for six years in a row, became the seventh largest US company.

Ken Lay's vision was bold. He decided the best way to dominate the energy industry was through e-commerce rather than the traditional leveraging of hard assets like pipelines. But as the execution of the game-changing strategy ran into challenges, Lay tried to cover up financial losses and difficulties that piled up—often through fraudulent accounting (the infamous off-balance-sheet deceits) and shredded documents. He hid the bad news and unethical accounting practices from the executive team, board, and investors. The board trusted him and never dug into the financials. Other stakeholders, including the auditors, employees, customers, and investment community, were convinced that this was a successful company.

Lay used his cult status and obscure reporting to create one of the greatest business disasters in history. At its peak, Enron was valued at $70 billion. By 2001, the company had failed, resulting in the largest bankruptcy in US history. Thousands of employees lost their jobs, investors lost their money, the accounting firm Arthur Andersen went out of business, the company was charged with fraud, and senior executives went to jail. Enron's spectacular rise and fall led to extensive congressional hearings and investigations. The Sarbanes-Oxley Act in 2002 and additional regulations by the stock exchanges were developed to address the specific corporate governance failings that occurred at Enron.

The regulations enacted after Enron's collapse can improve governance but cannot eliminate all the risks. Boards, executives, employees, and investors must be vigilant in overseeing operations, especially when there is a dominant CEO and opaque information. That was the lesson we learned from Enron.

But when Theranos happened we found out we didn't learn it well enough.

ELIZABETH HOLMES AND THERANOS

For a while, heralded entrepreneur Elizabeth Holmes pulled off one of the biggest, brashest fakes in recent business history. All was rosy for Theranos until a diligent journalist from the *Wall Street Journal*, John Carreyrou, uncovered the truth: Holmes, Theranos, and the technology the company was based on were frauds.

Just how did Holmes hoodwink the board and investors? Why didn't they sniff out the deception before things fell apart?

Holmes' desire to improve the world with faster, better blood tests caught the imagination of board members, investors, partners, and media alike. She claimed Theranos could complete a full range of tests with a drop or two of blood from a simple pinprick on the finger. The Theranos business model envisioned walk-in clinics and, ultimately, in-home testing. Holmes promised a brave new world and claimed her invention was "the most important thing humanity has ever built."

Holmes had a great story. She dropped out of Stanford University's school of Chemical Engineering at age nineteen with a passion to "discover something new, something mankind didn't know was possible to do." That story struck a nerve; Holmes was treated like a superstar. As the Theranos story spread, she was on the cover of *Forbes* and *Fortune*, was profiled in the *New Yorker*, and was featured on television. In the process, she amassed a net worth of around $4 billion.

Carreyrou, a Pulitzer Prize-winning investigative journalist with a nose for a good story, caught the scent of something amiss. He used his journalistic prowess to find out what was really going on—the technology did not work as claimed, and the truth was being covered up. The company was not using its own technology to conduct most of the blood tests, and fewer than 10 percent of the tests Theranos conducted were via one-drop finger pricks. His front-page *Wall Street Journal* exposé in 2015 questioned the accuracy of the Theranos lab results and suggested the company had cheated on tests related to lab certification.

The story kicked off a series of events that collapsed the business, fueled a devastating SEC investigation, and eventually led to criminal charges against Holmes. But not before a million blood tests had been run and some lives had been put in jeopardy.

Red flags should have been evident to the board much earlier than Carreyrou's tell-all story. In the formative days of Theranos, while media, partners, and investors were being courted by Holmes, telltale signs were piling up. Holmes refused to describe to anyone how the technology worked, including investors and the board, because she said it would compromise Theranos' competitive advantage. When the Walgreens team visited Theranos to qualify a partnership proposal and wanted to see the labs, they were denied access. And patients were ignored when they called Theranos to complain the tests were inaccurate.

In 2015, months before Carreyrou's story hit, government investigators were tracking the scent of fraud. The FDA sent investigators to the Theranos labs in Palo Alto and Newark, California. The Centers for Medicare and Medicaid, the group that regulates medical labs, discovered Theranos had bypassed internal quality-control protocols and that there were anomalies in Theranos test results that could put patients at risk for internal bleeding or stroke.

Holmes had control over every aspect of Theranos—she was founder, CEO, and chairwoman. To keep the lid on any sort of negative information slipping out of the company, she had established a culture of fear. One observer said she treated disagreement brutally. Secrecy was mandated, and employees who dared question the technology, quality control, or other aspects of the business were fired.

Holmes was a master at managing and massaging the information to convince others the technology worked. She pulled the wool over the eyes of top-flight investors. Marc Andreessen called her the next Steve Jobs. VC Draper Fisher Jurvetson invested, as did a bevy of high-net-worth investors.

She mesmerized the board. The Theranos board was composed of older white men, and their experience in health care was very limited. Members included two former US secretaries of state, Henry Kissinger and George Schultz; William Perry, former defense secretary; Sam Nunn, former US senator and chairman of the Armed Service Committee; and David Boies, superstar lawyer. Bill Frist, former senate majority leader and a former cardiovascular doctor, was the only one with medical experience. None of them saw through the lie.

Holmes avoided board confrontation and used a "velvet glove technique" with them, according to observers. When the board asked questions, she fed them obfuscating answers. When they recommended a course of action, she said yes but then did what she wanted.

Financial management had been an unforgivable mess from the beginning, and by 2017, Theranos still did not have a budgeting process and lacked auditable financial statements. Getting the Theranos books in shape for an audit proved to be a huge challenge. There were no reliable records of investors, how much they invested, and at what valuations. To complicate matters, no one had tracked fixed assets such as technology, equipment, and furniture. As external pressure on the company mounted, efforts to produce an accurate financial picture intensified. But it was too little, too late.

The FDA banned the use of Theranos' testing device. The SEC issued a damning ruling of fraud that included a fine and banned Holmes from serving as chief executive of a public company. In June 2018, Elizabeth Holmes and her COO were charged with multiple counts of conspiracy and fraud in federal court. This followed other extensive litigation that is likely to go on for years. In August 2018, the company announced it would cease to exist.

Holmes was expert at using her magnetic personality to get her way and kept nearly everyone in the dark about what was really going on. But Holmes had a special trait: she was willing to lie to make her vision come true. Eventually an alert journalist unpacked the lies. But why didn't the board know what was going on before it became front-page news? Why didn't they see through the smokescreen and act?

With a vigilant and prepared board, a leader should never succeed in such high-level deception. There are steps investors, employees, and the board should take to make sure that never happens.

SHARED RESPONSIBILITY

Iron-willed masters of change have personalities with sharp edges—important characteristics that set them apart. They are extremely hard driving and expect the people they work with to be the same. Each one challenges the status quo of business behavior and often breaks some rules to turn their vision into reality. Their entrepreneurial spirit makes them consummate at selling their ideas, and they have a charisma that opens doors and inspires followers. Their claimed capacity to deliver world-changing ideas generates passionate customers and resonates with employees looking for a champion, as well as with money-minded investors.

The innovative big shot is always the one in the limelight. They receive the accolades and get the front-page coverage. But they are not alone—investors and employees support them and make the CEO's vision a reality. And the board is complicit. A board that actively affirms a founder's good decisions can clear the way for even greater success. But without a board willing to provide clear guidance and say no at the right times, the change maker can send the company into a tail spin through poor decisions or behaviors that undermine the company. We believe that in the end, the revolutionary leader, board, employees, and investors are contributors to the enterprise's success or failure.

RED FLAGS FOR INVESTORS AND BOARD MEMBERS.

Here are some of the CEO red flags we heard from members of the board and others involved in governance:

- *Blinding dazzle—too-slick presentations and strict control of the agenda leave little or no room for alternate perspectives*

- *Secrecy—access to information and the ability to contact key people are blocked*

- *"Fire Me" challenge—CEO says, "If you don't like it, fire me," knowing full well there is not a succession plan in place*

- *Autocratic snubs—two styles of brush-off sometimes used in tandem:* hard freeze-out *where the CEO openly denies any other opinions or alternate actions, and* soft repulse *where the CEO says yes to a request to do something differently but subsequently does what they want*

- **Overconfidence**—*alarming disregard for alternate opinions and advice*

- **Compensation focus**—*extreme focus on pushing the board to increase compensation*

- **Insensitivity**—*thoughtless and total lack of respect for employees' feelings*

- **Executive exodus**—*senior execs leaving in droves or after a short stay*

- **Blind spots**—*CEO does not realize elements of business savvy and experience are missing from their repertoire*

- **Wimpy board**—*CEO influences board membership and procedures to minimize dissent and contrary opinions*

CHAPTER 3

LESSONS FROM BOLD BEHAVIORS

Energized, imaginative leaders make their marks in different ways. They can be ingenious creators of wealth, rule breakers that upend the status quo, or strong leaders armed with keen insights. They can also be liars or jerks.

This chapter distills the stories of chapter 2 and describes the qualities that make these larger-than-life disrupters both an opportunity and a challenge for everyone around them—employees, investors, and the boards charged with governing them. After that, in Part Two: Solving the Puzzle, we launch into the ways to address a leader's taxing temperament, stay productive and engaged in the face of subpar behavior, facilitate ease, and govern these agents of change.

BEHAVIORS OF DOMINANT VISIONARIES

We know ingenious business leaders can produce remarkable results. That is the reason difficult mavericks like Steve Jobs and Elon Musk are embraced by investors, employees, and boards of directors.

There are seven other noteworthy behaviors you find in industry-disrupting trailblazers.

1. SOMETIMES THEY LIE.

It happens all the time. In the process of building a company and bringing about change, leaders assure the public and investors they have developed a product, when in reality, it is still in formative stages and far from commercial readiness. Or, to build support, they claim a technology can do miraculous things when the truth is it can't—at least not in its current state. Others, to show progress, specify a commercial launch date even though they know the date is pure fiction—the development program is still underway and nowhere near completion, and no one really knows if and when it will be ready to launch.

Lying is an ethos common to many innovators. In Silicon Valley, it's referred to as *Fake it till you make it*.

Far too many innovators believe it is okay to bend the truth or lie in pursuit of their goals. But that can be dangerous. Warren Buffett, explaining his approach to business, said he and vice chairman Charlie Munger "have seen all sorts of bad corporate behavior, both accounting and operational, induced by the desire of management to meet Wall Street expectations. What starts as an 'innocent' fudge in order to not disappoint 'the Street'—say, trade-loading at quarter-end, turning a blind eye to rising insurance losses, or drawing down a 'cookie-jar' reserve—can become the first step toward full-fledged fraud."

Savvy, ethical visionaries know you must tell the truth. For them, this is a clear line that cannot be crossed. For others without that moral compass, the line is blurred. They don't discern the difference between truth and the fiction of what they want to believe.

Elizabeth Holmes layered lie on lie and, using her cult status and total control of information inside the company, hid the fact that Theranos technology could not deliver the promised performance. She kept telling people what she wanted the truth to be. But it was all made up. As a result, the company delivered inaccurate medical test results to patients and doctors, endangering lives and defrauding investors of almost a billion dollars. Theranos was done in by Holmes' propensity to lie, the board's lack of action to put an end to her deceit, and investors' lack of diligence.

Bending the truth and other forms of deception coexist easily when there is belief it is all done to help create a better world. Dan Ariely, professor of psychology and behavioral economics at Duke University, and someone who has studied Holmes' behavior at Theranos, has shown that good intentions make it easier to hide from the truth. He believes Holmes intended to create a world-changing innovation but resorted to deception when things did not go as planned.

Ariely backs up this claim with an experiment he ran showing that subjects can believe their lies are true, and fool a lie detector, if they are told their lies will be rewarded with donations to charity. In participants' minds, the lie is neutralized and forgiven if the outcome will be beneficial. The harsh reality is that some people, given the right conditions and mind-set, can convince themselves that lying is all right.

Lies are not good, but some are worse than others. Commercializing a technology or business model in the medical arena like Theranos has different risks than commercializing a new gaming software or phone app. Boards, executive teams, employees, and investors have the responsibility to ensure the facts presented are true. In the medical arena, and anywhere people's lives are at stake, the board and employees have an added responsibility to ensure safe and healthy outcomes.

All stakeholders—executives, employees, investors, and boards—need to recognize and accept the responsibility to fact-check even the most respected leader. During our interviews, we heard something that still resonates: "The board needs to build a code of conduct and be vigilant. Small lies are a slippery slope. *Fake it till you make it* mentality is the kiss of death."

2. POWERFUL PERSONALITIES CAN TURN INTO JERKS.

Charismatic firebrands are extremely purposeful in driving themselves and the people who work for them. They put everything into their quest to create something new. Often those leaders believe in the vision so deeply they become stubborn and rigid when challenged. They believe they know best and resort to bullying to quash any opposing viewpoints. That makes them difficult to work with, govern, or even talk to. Sometimes it makes them insufferable.

Self-entitlement was a trademark behavior of Steve Jobs. He berated and taunted anyone who crossed him or frustrated his plans. That created huge friction with his employees, executives, and partners. Many tolerated his outbursts and lived with his bad behavior. After all, he was the boss and was building a hugely successful company. Others sulked and tended to their wounded egos or left.

Being a jerk is not okay. It corrodes trust and destroys value. Reed Hastings, CEO of Netflix, says "Do not tolerate brilliant jerks. The cost to teamwork is too high." In addition, self-centered leaders who are cruel or rude often subject their organizations to potentially ruinous legal risks. Not only are they less likely to take advice from seasoned veterans, they are more likely to become embroiled in protracted litigation.

We may never know exactly what went down in the Uber board and company meetings while the company was dealing with Kalanick's jerk behaviors. But you can't help but wonder what could have been done earlier by the board and leadership team to avoid the pain.

Boards and executives need to get involved when they see jerkish behavior—even if it is from a stellar performer like Jobs or a trailblazer like Kalanick.

3. BRAININESS CAN HIDE GAPS.

Braininess is a prerequisite for a revolutionary change maker. They see things others have missed and are able to do things many cannot. Their intellectual prowess is a key ingredient in their vision and a large part of their charisma—especially if they are very young like Page and Holmes.

Intellectual precociousness can have a downside. Many big brains lack critical management experience and important social skills. They don't have all the tools required to make their vision a reality. It is the responsibility of the board and the management team to work in concert and fill the gaps, so the CEO's intrinsic smarts are complemented. This can take the shape of a seasoned manager that rounds out leadership and business judgment and minimizes the impact of an enfant terrible.

Adding Eric Schmidt to the Google leadership team to provide experienced supervision was a stroke of genius. Schmidt provided the management expertise and prior experience building an organization that was missing from Larry Page's repertoire. Facebook benefited in a similar manner by bringing in COO Sheryl Sandberg.

One can't help but wonder if supplementing some management expertise early on would have benefited Musk and avoided some of the turmoil at Tesla.

4. VISIONARIES ARE EXTREMELY TOUGH TASKMASTERS.

Hard-core leaders on a mission are compelled to achieve their goal and demand the highest level of performance. That can create a tense environment and daunting culture. Elon Musk, Steve Jobs, and many others are famous for handing out monumental demands peppered with ferocious criticism if performance is not to their liking.

Jeff Bezos created Amazon's high-pressure, excellence-only environment. Some employees seem to thrive on it. Others find the pressure too great and the pay too little.

Bezos is unlikely to change the high performance requirements for continued employment in Amazon. It is part of his formula for success. He created that culture to complement his vision of industry-dominating companies, and it has led Amazon to become a trillion-dollar juggernaut.

But Bezos prides himself on learning and adapting as he goes. The recent criticism of the tough work environment and low pay at Amazon spurred him to raise the minimum wage to fifteen dollars per hour. With the statement "We listened to our critics, thought hard about what we wanted to do, and decided we want to lead," Bezos and his board sent a strong signal to employees and competitors: Amazon will stick to the model of a demanding workplace but adapt as necessary to stay on top.

Demanding work environments and brilliant CEOs almost always go hand in hand. Boards may not quibble with that approach but should remain alert to ensure things do not get out of control. Otherwise they will be forced to deal with messes after the fact. In 2018, Musk pushed employees to extreme levels during the production ramping of Model 3. As a result, the board had to respond to allegations of harassment and improper dismissal. Martin Winterkorn, Volkswagen's CEO, was fired because he created an extreme company culture—described by *Der Spiegel* as "North Korea without labor camps"—that drove employees to create and install illegal software that cheated on vehicle emissions tests. Extreme demands are often a precursor to bad behaviors.

5. ETHICS CAN GET COMPROMISED
IN PURSUIT OF SUCCESS.

Kalanick's stint at Uber epitomizes why it is critical to establish, monitor, and enforce ethics guidelines through an active and diligent board. Without taking appropriate conduct seriously and making commitments to ethical business practices throughout the company, a toxic environment can grow.

Travis Kalanick was removed from the company he started due to his unruly behavior and the poisonous culture that he grew around him. Uber's crisis was not just Kalanick's failure. The board of directors did not fulfill their responsibility. There was a series of scandals, divisiveness, and harassment over several years. The board should have been actively and diligently monitoring and engaging in the ethical, cultural, strategic, and operational issues far earlier than it appears they did.

What happened at Uber is a prime example of the dysfunctional behavior that can develop when dominant visionaries combine with passive boards. At Uber, asymmetric power, a cult of personality, and opaque presentation of growing difficulties combined with the lack of active engagement of the board allowed problems to fester. In the end, the board had only one choice—terminate the CEO. But by then significant damage had been done. The board had to feel a little guilty. Even VC Benchmark admitted that "we are sorry that it has taken us so long to do the right thing."

Uber is not the only example of a company ousting their groundbreaking founder as a last resort. The board axed the founder of Zenefits a few years ago and, of course, the firing of Steve Jobs is well known. Wells Fargo's board tossed out CEO John Stumpf for creating and sustaining a culture that encouraged fraudulent activity and overcharges for hundreds of thousands of customers.

All too often, boards have been passive in their leadership and governance and ceded their responsibilities to chief executives and founders—especially with a hard-charging visionary at the helm. In many cases, the board became active and stepped in only when there was no other choice.

6. RULES GET BROKEN IN PURSUIT OF A PERCEIVED GREATER GOOD.

Actively challenging existing laws and regulations in the course of commercializing a new business model may be warranted to disrupt the status quo and create a new business. That's what rule breakers generally do.

Reid Hoffman, founder of LinkedIn, summed it up this way: "At PayPal . . . , we bent and broke some rules, but we did so because we believed we were working towards a better future for society at large. We felt that our actions were ethical because we believed that in the long run, we would convince the world to change its rules, and that the economy would be better off as a result. History demonstrates that we were right."

When a revolutionary leader drives a company against the status quo, the board and the executive team are complicit in the method of disruption as well as the outcome. Uber challenged regulators around the world. The company prided itself on the bold, pirate-like approach. But Uber ran into troubles as people fought back. The company was picketed, indicted, blocked from markets, and disparaged in the press. The board realized the financial costs and erosion of brand loyalty from confrontation were too great. Under new leadership and board control, the business changed its approach. But where was the board before?

By contrast, Spotify CEO Daniel Elk took a different and uncanny approach to challenging authority. Elk challenged the music industry, but he ensured Spotify did not act like a pirate intent on raiding, pillaging, and destroying the status quo. Instead, he chose to become an ally. This was risky because industry moguls thought Spotify's streaming app had the potential to totally disrupt the music industry the way Napster had tried to do. They hated Napster, and if Spotify was anything like Napster, it was a mortal enemy. Elk was aware of the antipathy. Right from the start, to assuage their concerns, he offered something Napster had not. Elk made the music industry his partner, sharing revenue and building a new channel for music consumption. His mantra was "We will save the music industry." It took a while, but over time they built trust and became collaborators.

It is important to be clear about what rules are okay to break and how they should be broken. The board members and executives we interviewed echoed the same message: the management team and the board share responsibility in that decision and its outcome. One summed it up well: "The board needs to specify the rules that can be broken—those that contribute to success of the innovation. And they need to be very specific about those that should not be broken. For instance, being mean to people or acting like a jerk should be out of bounds."

7. VISIONARIES CAN BE DANGEROUSLY UNPREDICTABLE.

Seemingly without warning, the behavior of a power-house genius can become uneven and counterproductive. They might break from their normal leadership role and do something offensive in public. Kalanick's recorded haranguing of an Uber driver showed he had a knack for that. Or the CEO might say, blog, or tweet things that are embarrassing and potentially destructive. Elon Musk is emblematic of this type of erratic behavior.

Musk has been rewarded handsomely for doing a lot of great things at Tesla. The board strongly supported him. In June 2018, the shareholders voted to keep him in the roles of both CEO and chairman because of his success. Then in August 2018, Musk surprised everyone by tweeting he wanted to take Tesla private. Now in addition to his role as CEO, chairman, and 20 percent shareholder, he was also a bidder for the company.

Finally, about three weeks later, after discussing it with the board, receiving criticism from many, and investigations by regulators for possible securities code violations (and likely many shareholder lawsuits), Musk reversed himself. The turmoil was further embarrassment for both Musk and the board and raised questions about his stability and leadership. The SEC slapped him with a $20 million fine and demanded he step down as chairman for three years.

Jeffrey Sonnenfeld, a professor of leadership and governance at Yale School of Management, reflected how this eroded Musk's reputation: "Tesla investors must realize that they have a panicky, erratic, possibly self-destructive CEO at the helm. No CEO is ever this confused and confusing." That may be a bit harsh, given what we know about other change-making chief executives, but the 2018 events brought board changes and increased the call for Tesla to hire a chief operating officer to help Musk, act as a stabilizing force, and bring strengths that Musk does not seem to possess.

Unexpected actions surprise the board, confuse company leadership, and undermine investor confidence. It is important to have clear guidelines about what are acceptable and unacceptable behaviors. Otherwise, the rule breaker makes the rules.

AGES AND STAGES

Companies evolve. Many dominant visionaries were also founders of their start-up companies, and there were no corporate structures or processes in place as the companies began. This architecture was developed as these companies grew, from a few employees, to dozens, and to hundreds or thousands.

From infancy to adolescence, each stage of growth creates new challenges. As companies mature from sole entrepreneur to a small core of employees or partners, to the first venture capital investment, and then to a public company, there is often little professional development for the required leadership skills. Historically, this evolution and growth took place over many years or even decades, so many CEOs learned on the job. In today's compressed timeframes, for many recent start-ups, the growth took months or only a few years.

Meanwhile, in parallel, the board has its own evolution. The executive team and board's role changes from its initial formation as a private company with no investors, to a company with a small number of angel or venture investors (and a small board), to a public company with responsibilities to a broader set of shareholders and other stakeholders. Internal controls along with other organizational systems and structures and a strong active, independent, and qualified board of directors are always needed as companies make this transition from a sole entrepreneurship to a professionally managed company. When the company is led by a founder who is often incendiary, this is particularly important.

Talented, assertive visionary leaders are confident people with strong ambitions and are almost always

MAVERICK LEADERS CAN BE MANY THINGS

- *Brilliant in certain, but not all, areas of business*

- *Powerful personalities that can be role models or turn into jerks*

- *People who compromise ethics in pursuit of success*

- *Rule breakers who claim they do it in pursuit of a perceived greater good*

- *Tough taskmasters that push people and culture to extremes*

- *Unpredictable and capable of undermining confidence and stakeholder values*

- *Liars with a mantra of "fake it till you make it"*

absolutely convinced they are right. The challenge for executives, employees, investors, and board members is how much trust to place in the change maker. Often the company is created on a compelling vision that is closely coupled with the founder. That breeds loyalty and conformity with the leader's decisions. Staying focused on the long-term value of the corporation can be difficult with these significant competing interests and pressures. Along the entire evolution of the company, a fundamental responsibility of executives, investors, and boards is to independently ask when this ingenious leader is right and when they may be wrong—and what should be done about it.

PREVENTIVE MEDICINE

Every trailblazing CEO has their own peculiar trove of braininess, power dynamics, organizational savvy, ethical compass, and leadership style.

If the integrity of the company or the responsibility to shareholders and society is at risk, investors, employees, management, and the board must shoulder responsibility for the consequences of inaction, delayed action, or incorrect action. Theranos' board and investors tacitly supported Holmes' big bet on an unproven technology—they sat back and waited to see what would happen. That resulted in catastrophic value destruction. It can happen in any company.

There's a better way. Even better than waiting until the ingenious industry disrupter acts, the board should define behaviors that are out of bounds and clearly map out the board roles and the triggers and processes for assessment, evaluation, and governance. The executive team's responsibilities include informing the board of key issues and keeping intact a positive company culture. Meanwhile, astute investors should be active and demand prudent governance processes, and watch for telltale signs of opportunities and problems.

Behaviors are not carved in stone. The tendencies of these imaginative and volatile leaders can change and shift over time. That can be good or bad news depending on what behaviors are emerging. In any event, the board should be alert and see when a transition is occurring. A change in the visionary's behavior may require a shift in the board's strategy and actions.

DEFINING SOLUTIONS

In Part Two: Solving the Puzzle, we deal with governance options to avoid the creation of the brainy jerk and to prevent other bad behaviors. We also describe approaches to enhance the positive outcomes a dominant visionary can generate.

Here are some questions we will address.

- How do you ensure that proper governance does not demotivate an inspired genius?
- Is founder control of the voting shares a good idea?
- What actions keep a governing genius from becoming a brainy jerk or worse?

- How can you see what is going on inside the company before a toxic culture evolves or serious problems arise?

And we will address this overarching question: *How do you know if, when, and how to intervene?*

PART TWO

SOLVING THE PUZZLE

Stakeholders are involved with ingenious leaders in various ways and to different degrees. Employees work with and around the visionary and within the company culture they create. To a very great extent, the leader's performance dictates their income and conditions of employment. Executives share the same environment with the added challenge of frequent, direct, and often contentious interactions regarding how to run the company. Partners in the company's value chain deal with the dominating leadership and exacting demands. Investors bet on the commanding innovator to make great things happen and have a stake in ensuring that the leader and company operate legally, ethically, and at the highest level of performance—they want their bet to pay off.

All these stakeholders try to find effective ways to work with and help an inspired, change-driven leader. But the board of directors sits at the center of responsibility. The success or failure of a dominant visionary is tightly tied to the board's actions—sometimes because of what they do and other times because of what they don't do.

Part One described how dominant visionaries create huge opportunities and pose unusual challenges. Now, in Part Two, we address the best ways to deal with the realities of a demanding rule breaker. Chapter 4: Mastering the Basics: Board Roles and Responsibilities describes the building blocks all companies need for governance. The chapter also shows how boards have become more active and have improved performance. Chapter 5: Keys to Governing a Dominant Visionary presents the seven things a board needs to do to support the ingenious CEO's execution of the vision. We provide options for key stakeholders in Chapter 6: Strategies for VCs, Executives, Employees, and Investors. Chapter 7: All Together Now lays out how to engage with a visionary and govern so the board and all stakeholders succeed.

CHAPTER 4

MASTERING THE BASICS: BOARD ROLES AND RESPONSIBILITIES

Just as sure as the CEO's role is to lead, the board's is to assist, guide, and enable them to build a great sustainable company. This chapter presents best-in-class basic governance practices for every company. Chapter 5 describes the additional things required for effective governance by companies with inventive and overbearing CEOs.

BUILDING BLOCKS

Boards have three core roles: accountability, senior level staffing and evaluation, and strategic oversight. The board's role in each is to supervise rather than be an active participant in the design, implementation, or management of the functions.

CORE BOARD ROLES AND RESPONSIBILITIES

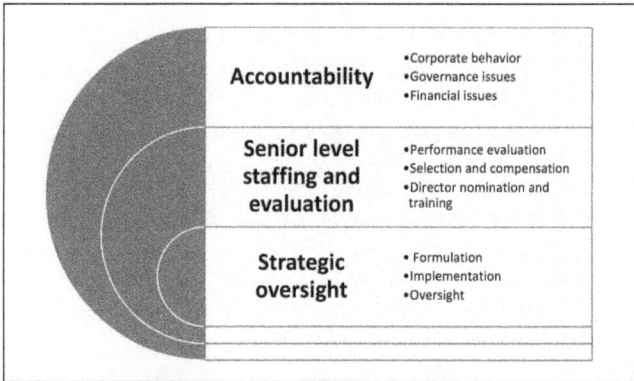

Accountability	• Corporate behavior • Governance issues • Financial issues	
Senior level staffing and evaluation	• Performance evaluation • Selection and compensation • Director nomination and training	
Strategic oversight	• Formulation • Implementation • Oversight	

Source: Adapted from M. J. Epstein and M. J. Roy, Strategic Management of Information for Boards, Society of Management Accountants of Canada and American Institute of Certified Public Accountants, Inc., 2007.

ACCOUNTABILITY

Boards of directors have an obligation to ensure corporate systems and structures effectively enforce accountability and ethical behavior. Accountability encompasses financial issues, corporate behavior, and governance issues.

ACCOUNTABILITY RESPONSIBILITIES

ACCOUNTABILITY	COVERAGE
Financial Systems	• Internal controls • Financial compliance systems • Disclosure processes
Corporate Behavior	• Codes of ethics • Other compliance systems • Policies that impact the various stakeholders of the corporation
Governance	• Evaluation and monitoring of corporate governance practices • Board performance

When boards fail to provide oversight, the consequences can be costly. Volkswagen stumbled badly when it installed the emission-testing "defeat device" in eleven million cars. It cost the company more than $20 billion, severely damaged their brand, and caused the resignations of board members and senior leaders.

The problem originated with VW's culture, which encouraged cheating. But the lack of strong internal controls let the fraud continue for ten years, from 2006 to 2015. Chairman of the Board Hans Dieter Pötsch admitted in 2015 that "there was a tolerance for breaking the rules" and that the decision to cheat on the emission tests was made ten years earlier in a climate of lax ethical standards after the company realized that it could not meet US clean-air standards legally.

SENIOR LEVEL STAFFING AND EVALUATION

The selection, evaluation, and compensation of the CEO and senior level executives is an important responsibility of corporate boards. This includes overseeing the development of the performance evaluation and compensation systems, succession planning, and the recruitment and development of both senior executives and the board of directors.

SENIOR LEVEL STAFFING AND EVALUATION

SENIOR STAFFING AND EVALUATION	COVERAGE
Development of Performance Evaluation and Compensation Systems	• Reviewing and approving corporate and senior executive goals for their evaluation and compensation • Performance evaluation, senior executive selection and compensation, and directors' nomination and training
Succession Planning	• Senior executive selection • Determining and approving the compensation of senior executives • Development of a succession plan
Senior Executive and Board Development	• Continuing educational needs • Directors' nomination including selection, nomination, and qualification • Compensation of board directors

When a corporation encounters a crisis, there is always a search for someone to blame and, often, someone to fire—the "bad apple" who corrupted others and is ultimately responsible for the problem. In 2016, Wells Fargo Bank's CEO announced that over the previous five years they had fired fifty-three hundred employees for "engaging in improper sales practices" and fraudulent activities. Basically, the CEO said that there were fifty-three hundred bad apples that had caused the problem.

The problem at Wells Fargo was not bad apples. The barrel was bad. Systems and incentives had been established that encouraged bank employees to increase sales and profitability by cross-selling—enticing existing customers to add more bank services. Under intense pressure to hit lofty sales targets set by Wells Fargo management, employees resorted to cheating. They opened two million accounts without the customers' knowledge or permission, and in some cases, employees transferred money between customer accounts without authorization.

When this fraud was detected, Wells was hit with large fines and lawsuits. Since 2016, Wells has paid more than $1.5 billion in fines to regulators and over $600 million to resolve lawsuits. The federal government's congressional hearings showed unusually strong bipartisan condemnation of Wells Fargo's executives, charging management with "gutless leadership." During the hearings, Congressman Brad Sherman said, "You took fifty-three hundred good Americans and turned them into felons."

The board had a clear responsibility to provide oversight of senior executives. When more than five thousand employees are fired, one can reasonably ask whether the senior executives and board members should have been fired instead of employees who were operating under an incentive system and pressures designed and overseen by the senior leadership. At AMP, the Australian financial services company that systematically overcharged customers and misled regulators, the chairman, CEO, and three board members resigned or were let go.

Headstrong leaders often resist developing a management replacement bench because they consider themselves irreplaceable.

We recall our experience with a board that repeatedly asked the CEO for a succession plan, but none was ever delivered. The CEO claimed that he had no plans to leave—or die—so no succession plan was necessary. This headstrong leader also believed that no one could replace him effectively. He had founded the company, led it for many years, and was the central force in its success.

The board had a serious dilemma. They were upset that the CEO would not follow the board's guidance on this critical issue and that he seemed to delight in challenging them. Yet they did not want the CEO to depart now and agreed that he was critical to the company's success.

With guidance, the board decided to tell the CEO that they were going to develop their own succession plan with or without the CEO's participation. The board determined the required qualifications for a new CEO and evaluated existing senior management. They also developed lists of potential external candidates.

When the dust settled, the CEO accepted their actions, and the board had a solid succession plan.

This was not an ideal succession planning process because it excluded the CEO. But the board rightly determined that they could not permit the recalcitrance of the CEO to put the company at risk by failing to have an effective succession plan. We cheered how they stood up to the challenge.

When Martin Sorrell, founder of WPP, a behemoth multinational advertising and public-relations company, was forced out after allegations of personal misconduct, the board was sent scrambling because there was not a succession plan for Sorrell. Lack of planning for the replacement of an imaginative and potentially irascible chief executive who not only runs the company but is the founder is a major mistake.

STRATEGIC OVERSIGHT

Boards are entrusted with the responsibility to oversee development and implementation of the company's mission, values, and strategy. This stewardship includes examining the people, processes, culture, and activities required to preserve and enhance the long-term value and success of the corporation.

There are three components of strategic oversight: strategy formulation, strategy implementation, and strategy monitoring.

STRATEGIC OVERSIGHT

STRATEGIC OVERSIGHT	COVERAGE
Strategy Formulation	• Reviewing and approving risk policies • Strategic direction and plans • Major capital investments and divestitures
Strategy Implementation	• Adopting a strategic planning process • Overseeing major capital expenditures
Strategy Monitoring	• Reviewing the strategy implementation process and its success • Reviewing and approving annual budgets

Strategic oversight may sound like an intellectual exercise. However, it has important operational consequences. On April 24, 2013, the collapse of the Rana Plaza building near Dhaka, Bangladesh, killed more than eleven hundred garment workers who were producing apparel for many of the world's more prominent retailers, including JC Penney, Walmart, The Children's Place, and Benetton. Being the deadliest disaster in the industry's history, it also highlighted an important corporate governance challenge that had not received attention. Leading retailers could no longer assume that labor and environmental policies were being enforced by others in their supply chains and that the factory inspection and audit programs were sufficient. Boards were compelled to step up to the responsibility, ensuring safety was not squandered in the pursuit of profits and protecting the interests of the corporation and its stakeholders.

One of the continual board challenges is balancing the responsibility of strategic oversight without micromanaging.

A board we know was presented with a well-developed proposal by the firebrand chief executive and senior leadership to build a massive new manufacturing facility in Brazil. The CEO's team had been working on the proposal for many months and presented a compelling argument for approval of this billion-dollar facility. As is often the case, the detailed PowerPoint proposal was presented as an initiative that was critical for future corporate success; no alternatives were to be considered. When some board members challenged some assumptions and questioned parts of the analysis, the CEO was indignant. He said he and his team had spent months on this and were confident that this was the only proper course of action. He went on to say he did not need arguments from a board, only approval. When the board requested a delay to develop alternative approaches, the CEO became enraged. "Is the board with me or not?" The board answered forcefully: the investment was nixed, and the CEO was replaced.

Frankly, that is an uncommon outcome. More often than not, boards acquiesce to leaders' demands. There is a deeply rooted reluctance to disturb the typically collegial relationship with the CEO. The GE board largely followed the chairman's lead during the reign of Jack Welch and Jeff Immelt; dissenting voices were seldom heard. A newcomer to the board was surprised by the lack of debate. He asked a more senior director to describe the role of a GE board member. "Applause," the older director answered.

CONTINUING EVOLUTION OF CORPORATE GOVERNANCE

Board responsibilities continue to evolve over time. For most of business history, corporate governance was within the control of one owner or a small ownership group. Not until the twentieth century did large, widely held corporate structures develop. That led to a separation of ownership, in the form of shareholders, and control via the management team and board of directors. Governing was now left primarily to the discretion of the senior executives as agents of the owners or to the owners themselves.

Though there were numerous regulations throughout the twentieth century to address corporate reporting, the stock market, and the issuance of securities, very little was done to regulate boards of directors and their control and responsibilities. It is only recently that there has been extensive interest in broadening the roles and responsibilities of boards of directors through various regulations by governments and stock exchanges and through case law.

Though there has been some debate over whether corporations should be primarily focused on the interests of only the shareholders rather than all stakeholders (often referred to as *shareholder versus stakeholder primacy*), there is no requirement that corporations focus solely on shareholders. Boards of directors should govern with the long-term interests of their corporations. Companies are embracing that idea. "It's because companies try to act in the interest of their shareholders that the public is distrusting of large institutions and corporations," said Brian Chesky, CEO of Airbnb. "Companies have a responsibility to society," said Chesky, who has been signing tax agreements with local authorities and imposing tighter regulations on Airbnb hosts as a way to better serve stakeholders.

This has become more relevant as various shareholders' and stakeholders' interests diverge and as even various shareholder groups have different interests and time horizons. Some shareholders hold shares for only days while others hold them for decades. With more than 70 percent of market value held by institutional owners, focus shifts to the long-term interests of the corporation.

When activist investors show interest in a company—usually long before they make a bid—it is a red flag and a call to action for directors. Typically, the board swings into action very quickly to determine the merits of the demands and conduct analysis to craft a plan. The CEO is part of the planning, but the board analysis and activities go beyond typical board involvement.

Boards have continued to change and grow to accommodate the new responsibilities, adapt to the dynamic business environment, and develop new approaches to improve performance. Recognizing that being passive participants on a CEO-run board is risky, board members have become more vigilant and far more actively engaged exercising their responsibilities.

A continuing challenge for boards is to determine when they should be collaborating and partnering with the CEO, when they should be intervening, leading, and exercising their overall control of the corporation, and when they should be staying out of the way to enable the leadership team to lead more effectively. No matter which path they choose, each requires an active rather than passive board to ensure that the best long-term interests of the corporation are primary. Currently, most corporate leaders and regulators have come to recognize that the basic building blocks of governance are necessary but not sufficient. A more active and empowered board of directors is critical for the successful long-term interests of the corporations and its stakeholders.

IMPORTANCE OF ACTIVE BOARDS

To set the stage, let's look again at the Enron debacle, this time from the perspective of the role the board played.

After being touted as one of the most innovative and profitable corporations in the US in the 1990s,

Enron became the largest bankruptcy in US history in 2001. The members of the Enron board of directors demonstrated excessive trust in CEO Ken Lay, considered a rock star in the business world, and the senior management team. At the CEO's request, the board suspended the company's conflict-of-interest policy to permit the CFO to establish special-purpose entities to partner with Enron. This set the stage for a bevy of financial mischief and allowed the CFO to earn millions. The board trusted the CEO even though the members did not fully understand the complex financial transactions or financial statements. Their trust was based on a respect for his business acumen and the continued rise in the share price.

Even when the board had doubts and wondered whether it should challenge the CEO, the significant support of Wall Street and of the press and Lay's prominence in the community dissuaded them from action. They had comfort and felt validated as the stock price continued to rise—until it no longer did, and the company filed for bankruptcy. It turns out that the financial statements Lay provided were largely misleading and fraudulent. Numerous senior executives were convicted of felonies and served lengthy prison sentences.

The Enron story is one of the best examples of the importance of active and conscientious boards, what can happen when a board fails to act, and some of the unique challenges a board faces when a charismatic, strong-willed boss is in charge.

STEPPING UP TO NEW CHALLENGES

On the heels of the Enron bankruptcy, much has changed for corporate boards. This includes the passage of various regulations, including the Sarbanes-Oxley Act of 2002, along with new rules at most of the major stock exchanges throughout the world that further define and increase responsibility, governance, transparency, and overall accountability of board members. Thankfully, the rise of this domineering class of leaders, generating both corporate successes and failures, has created new awareness and activity in boards.

As a result, boards have generated new approaches to improve performance. Some of these are critical in determining the overall composition of the board and the needed qualifications for individual board members. Others are improved processes needed to upgrade effective governance. All of them augment the core board roles and responsibilities (basic building blocks) and are important additions for governing dominant visionaries.

8 KEYS TO SUPERIOR BOARD PERFORMANCE

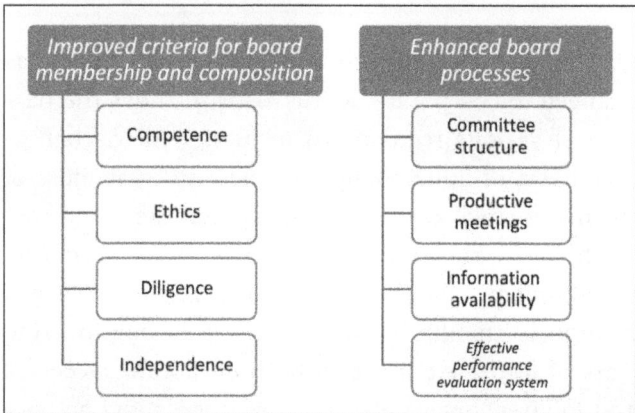

Improved criteria for board membership and composition	Enhanced board processes
Competence	Committee structure
Ethics	Productive meetings
Diligence	Information availability
Independence	*Effective performance evaluation system*

Source: Adapted from M. J. Epstein and M. J. Roy, Measuring and Improving the Performance of Corporate Boards, Society of Management Accountants of Canada, 2002.

IMPROVED CRITERIA FOR BOARD MEMBERSHIP AND COMPOSITION

For much of corporate history, board members were chosen by the CEO based on personal relationships and affiliations and they were longtime friends of the chief executive. They were often lacking in the skills and knowledge necessary, expected to vote with the CEO, and unable to provide the independence needed to challenge the CEO on critical issues. This practice still exists to a lesser extent today but is no longer generally acceptable.

Active boards build in four qualities essential for board members to engage effectively as counselors, vigilant monitors, and skeptical judges for long-term corporate success.

Competence: Board members should be elected based on skills, knowledge, and competencies. It is desirable to have diversity in experience, education, and background to develop a foundation for a thorough discussion of board issues. Needed skills and competencies often evolve over time as technologies, processes, customers, products, and the business environment change. These shifts often demand alterations in board composition to adapt to the new business environment.

Board composition significantly influences proper execution of board processes, including how the board prepares, deliberates, and decides.

Boards with dominant visionaries should be especially careful if the inspired, dominant CEO played a significant role in choosing the board members. They may not have the necessary experience, personality to complement other board members, and inclination to challenge the CEO when necessary. Board members know the power of the right composition. One told us, "The key to success with a strong leader is to have a process for putting together a strong board. Our innovative founder had huge respect for the board because they had very relevant experience. We had senior, experienced, mature experts on our board."

Ethics: The development and maintenance of an ethical culture is a primary responsibility of both the senior management team and the board of directors through its oversight. This responsibility is not always managed well. There have been too many examples of companies that suffered significant financial distress or collapse due to ethical violations. To step up to that challenge and ensure ethics are not compromised in pursuit of success, active boards take a hard look at the integrity and culture as the company develops, especially with a controlling and influential CEO at the helm. To protect against costly and embarrassing missteps like Uber's, active boards with dominant visionaries ensure that strong ethical foundations are established and monitored for both the board and the corporation. There is zero tolerance for unethical behavior on the part of the CEO, employees, or board.

Diligence: The days when being a board member meant just showing up at quarterly meetings and supporting whatever the CEO proposed are long past. Today, board members are expected to conscientiously prepare for each board meeting, engage actively in the discussions at the meeting, and vote based on their own independent judgment. This more active valence dramatically increases the time board members spend on preparation and meetings and reduces the number of boards that members are typically involved in at one time (a practice known as *overboarding*). Conscientious diligence is particularly critical in companies led by dominant visionaries. A hard-driving leader with voting superiority or a charismatic personality can overpower deliberations of board members who are not diligent and strong in exercising their own power. *Independence:* Independence is one of the cornerstones of good corporate governance. Board members are required to place the long-term interests of the corporation and its various stakeholders above the interests of the board, the senior management team, or the CEO. There have been extensive discussions and research on the pros and cons of whether the roles of the CEO and board chair should be combined or separated. There are many with strong views on these subjects. Andy Grove, CEO of Intel, weighed into the debate this way: "The separation of the two jobs goes to the heart of the conception of a corporation. Is a company a sandbox for the CEO, or is the CEO an employee? If he's an employee, he needs a boss, and that boss is the board. The chairman runs the board. How can the CEO be his own boss?" The snapshots in chapter 2 show how dominant CEOs can unduly influence the board through charisma. Boards often err in being too agreeable, especially if the CEO had a significant role in choosing members. Board members must avoid conflicts, be willing to challenge the CEO and other board members, and vote based on their due diligence and best judgment rather than based on relationships.

ENHANCED BOARD PROCESSES

In addition to strict requirements about who can serve, responsible boards develop ways to safeguard the organization. The choices made about the leadership of the board, the way it is organized and operates, and how the agenda is set are critical factors for success.

There are four processes active boards include for superior performance.

1. ***Committee structure:*** Boards commonly have at least three standing core committees—audit, compensation, and nominating or governance. Other standing or temporary committees are added to address key company issues such as technology, innovation, or risk or safety. Strong, active, and well-informed committee members and chairs have become important ingredients to working well with a dominant CEO—either supporting their vision or, when the circumstances require it, standing up to them.

2. ***Productive meetings:*** Determining what topics the board will discuss and how they will
be presented has a major impact on meeting
outcomes. CEOs often bias data presented to
the board to support their point of view. Or
they limit the conversation. Carlos Ghosn,
the autocratic CEO of Nissan, disliked having questions or dissenting opinions raised in
board meetings. Robust debate was quashed,
and meetings typically lasted twenty minutes.

   To avoid CEO control, the board chair or
lead director typically sets agenda and spec-
ifies both the content and process of those
meetings. This is especially important for
companies with dominant visionaries where
meetings can become merely presentations
by the CEO with little opportunity for discussion or questions. Active boards are vigilant to
check on the quality of information presented
at meetings and generate contrary opinions to
ensure balanced and carefully considered discussions and decisions.

3. ***Information availability:*** Legally, the board
has the equivalent of subpoena powers to
access any and all information in the company.
Aggressive pursuit of essential information
eliminates any opaqueness introduced by a
CEO. Active boards have access to independent
sources related to all aspects of the company,

including conversations with employees to better understand the challenges to the CEO and the corporation. Netflix requires board members to sit in on several executive meetings to get firsthand exposure to what is going on in the company and the information being used to make decisions. "You see a different level of dynamic of the executive team. You really see how different individuals contribute . . . and you see the dynamic with the CEO. You see how the topics that have been discussed, resolved, and reported on in a board meeting actually got processed," commented one director. To augment the board's perspective, contrary opinions and outside information should be sought when needed. Active boards withhold decisions until adequate information is received. It is a red flag when information is withheld or access to management is curtailed.

4. *Effective performance evaluation systems:*
Boards often delegate the development and implementation of performance evaluation systems to the senior management teams. Active boards maintain watchful supervision and oversight. With a domineering CEO, it is particularly important since performance evaluations and incentives are sometimes abused to support the CEO's followers and weed out dissidents. It is also important that systems for assessment are extended to

evaluate the performance of both individuals and the overall board. Too often, company boards have outdated systems and are lax in rigorously evaluating their own performance.

Source: Adapted from M. J. Epstein and M. J. Roy, Measuring and Improving the Performance of Corporate Boards, Society of Management Accountants of Canada, 2002.

The basic building blocks of governance and improved methods of active board roles work well for most companies. All of them are essential for an organization with a dominant visionary. However, they are not enough to deal with the full range of challenges and opportunities an unruly genius generates. The next chapter describes the additional key ingredients needed to function with, govern, and support an extraordinary and highly difficult CEO.

WHERE TO START:
BUILDING BLOCKS AND ACTIVE BOARDS

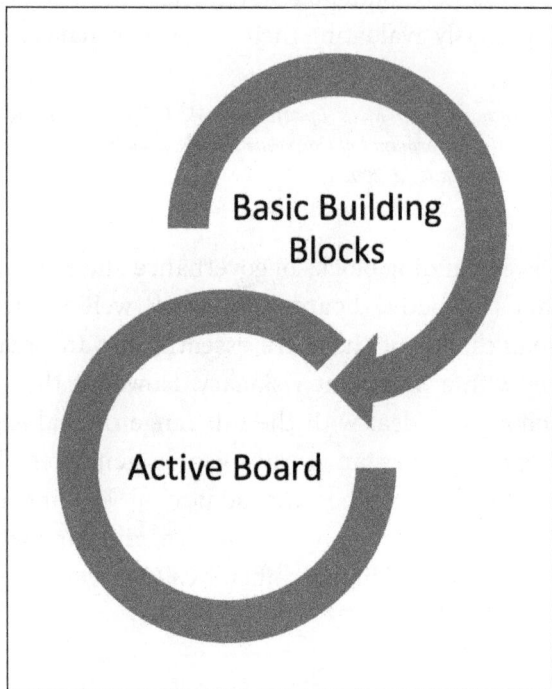

CHAPTER 5

KEYS TO GOVERNING A DOMINANT VISIONARY

All boards are tasked with developing corporate governance and strategic oversight that foster an ethical, responsible, and successful culture and provide checks and balances on the CEO. Boards with a strong-willed change maker at the helm have the additional challenge of supporting the freewheeling CEO's entrepreneurial endeavors. They ensure that the CEO's brilliance and drive to create something new does not lead to dysfunctional behavior.

In response to the cautionary tales we shared in previous chapters, corporate boards have developed techniques to handle genius CEOs and the challenges they present. There are three keys to governing a dominant visionary: activities taken at the early stages of the board development, ongoing board governance, and board interventions.

3 KEYS TO GOVERNING
A DOMINANT VISIONARY

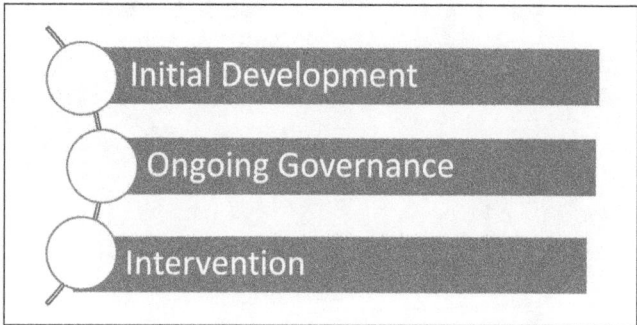

Initial Development

Ongoing Governance

Intervention

GETTING STARTED

Initial development has three interlocking pieces: board composition, board practices, and very importantly, evaluation of the CEO.

The first thing every board does is add members and build governance processes. Chapter 4 described the elements of an active, balanced board and the leading-edge core corporate governance practices.

There is an additional step when dealing with a torchbearing CEO who tends to make and break rules. The board evaluates the leader's management style and the implications it has on governance. "Learning to be thoughtful" about the CEO was how one director put it.

As members of the board, you need enough insight to answer two questions.

1. *What behaviors can you expect from the visionary?*
2. *When do you need to stay out of the way and where should you build buffers?*

INITIAL DEVELOPMENT PIECES

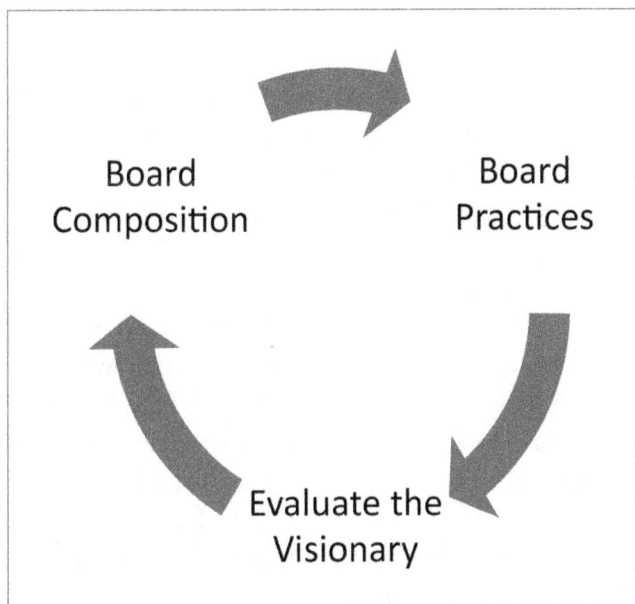

Board Composition

Board Practices

Evaluate the Visionary

Armed with the assessment, the board develops a customized plan that adds or subtracts members over time to round out the board composition to fit the CEO. They tailor governance processes to the chief executive's specific characteristics and the challenges and opportunities they will generate. Many boards duck this critical responsibility. They hope the basic governing processes they have put in place will suffice. That's a dangerous move—especially with a maverick in charge.

Recounting years of experience with multiple boards, one veteran said, "I am always amazed that boards with very smart, experienced people act dumb. The reason is they become insular. You need to have the right people on the board, individuals with differing, valuable perspectives. You need a mix of people, so you get proper representation of different business mind-sets—some that are aggressive and some that are cautious. The board also needs outside objective observers to check itself. The Theranos board composition should have been a red flag. They lacked businesspeople with relevant business experience. For example, an ex-CEO would have made a good contrarian."

Nasty experiences at Theranos, Enron, and Uber, and other governance implosions with ingenious pioneers, show how sitting back and assuming everything will be okay can be a costly mistake. With board composition, it pays to be proactive and wise, like John Doerr's decision at Google to add experienced leadership to the executive ranks.

PROFILING YOUR DISRUPTER-IN-CHIEF

There are several behavioral characteristics that we recommend boards and other stakeholders use to evaluate and understand the inspired, dominant leader and cater their approach to maintain productive collaboration.

Brainiac quotient: All dominant visionaries are brainy but not in the same way. Some are technology whiz kids like Page and Musk; others, like Jeff Bezos, are on the top end of the brain scale at designing disruptive business models. It is essential that you know what type of genius you are dealing with.

Gaps in experience or skills: Braininess does not make up for experience, and even very brainy people do some things better than others. Larry Page's brilliance was nicely complemented by Eric Schmidt's business savvy and experience. Adding retail experience to Apple's board helped Steve Jobs when he created the Apple Store. You need a solid appraisal of the strengths and weaknesses that characterize your pioneering leader.

Propensity to break rules: All dominant visionaries are rule breakers, but some are prone to going to extremes. That is a red flag and requires guidelines on what is out of bounds, and possibly processes to track and manage what gets broken. Travis Kalanick is the poster child in this category. His board did not act early enough to curtail his counterproductive rule-breaking behaviors.

Tendency to be a jerk: There is a spectrum of jerkiness. Obstreperous behavior once in a while is not uncommon and probably deserves little concern. Rampant jerkiness is a red flag. It is not the kiss of death, but it complicates and possibly compromises the pathfinder's ability to build collaborative teams and establish partnerships to drive the enterprise. Over the years, Apple's board wrestled with Jobs' jerkiness and its effects. We want you to look for signs of jerkiness.

Ferocity: Being a tough taskmaster is the norm for a fire-breathing CEO—changing the world requires a highly energized approach to everything. But too much toughness can create a monster leader and a culture where aggressive behavior is expected from everyone all the time. Left unattended, that leads to the feral behaviors seen at Uber. Properly managed it can be an asset. Jeff Bezos' high-pressure environment at Amazon has contributed to spectacular growth and nonstop innovation. But it is a delicate balance—some employees are comfortable with the intensity while others find the environment corrosive. You need to gauge the ferocity of your dominant visionary and know what turns them into a tyrant.

Impulsiveness: A headstrong CEO's tendency to jump off the rails and do something unexpected, illegal, or in bad taste is cause for concern for everyone. Elon Musk's escapades have upset shareholders and regulators, and, while Musk seemed unconcerned, the board probably wished they could have managed that better and earlier. Realizing the need to get more involved, the Tesla chairwoman recently adjusted board composition to bring new perspectives. Every board and all stakeholders need to get a handle on what can set off the boss and trigger reckless behaviors and enable the governance mechanisms to curtail destructive actions.

Ethical compass: Brilliant founders and leaders got their job by being rule breakers. They thrive on challenging orthodoxy. But how far will they push boundaries? And which boundaries? Taking a snapshot at one point in time and drawing conclusions is not wise. You need to observe the firebrand's behavior and penchant for hewing the ethical line over time to get a realistic and fair understanding.

VISIONARY PROFILE

Brainiac quotient

Gaps in experience or skills

Propensity to break rules

Tendency to be a jerk

Ferocity

Impulsiveness

Ethical compass

Having worked with a firebrand CEO, one person with years of board experience stressed the importance of understanding a disrupter's unique wiring: "Boards need to better understand the visionary leader, how special they are, and what makes them tick. Brilliant CEOs like this are inherently hard to read, but they are an asset that can increase in value with the right approach."

Armed with good insights, you and other members of the board will be able to tailor governance, including where and how to get involved, and when to stay out of the way.

VOTING CONTROL

A board should be especially alert and carefully tailor their approach when the creative, disrupting visionary founder has voting control. There are examples of voting control through the dual class structure being successful, especially in the initial stages of a company. Mark Zuckerberg's voting control enabled him to resist strong board pressure to sell the company in the early years of Facebook. His dominance of the board produced a company with spectacular growth and profitability.

On the other hand, asymmetric power can frustrate board oversight and cause problems. It contributed to the disaster at Theranos, and it was difficult for Uber's board to push out CEO Travis Kalanick even after he became a major liability, because he controlled the board through the dual class structure. In those cases, the board would have benefited from an approach tailored specifically to the CEO's leadership style.

Some boards set an end date for the multiple tiers of stock that create asymmetric power. One proposal that has been floated is to use a seven-year sunset that would restore the capital structure to one share, one vote. This is the direction Snap, Blue Apron Group, and other start-ups have taken. It gives the founder voting control during the initial growth period and avoids making them ruler for life. And some founders, like Bezos at Amazon, have done well without a controlling share. Whatever the approach, the board's decision on share control is a serious matter. The question of control can become crucial when a company gets into trouble. And the board owns the outcome.

Things can change fast with an innovative, high-energy CEO. The board and governance processes need to continually adapt. We think learning what has worked well and what hasn't, as well as updates on the visionary's behavior profile, should be part of the board's regular agenda so they can refine board composition and processes to better govern, support, and coach.

ONGOING GOVERNANCE

Governing a potentially unruly powerhouse is tough and something most board members have never done. You are in a small minority if you have experience governing or living with a groundbreaking force-of-nature CEO. The challenges of governing are different if you have a creative firebrand; issues intensify and heat up at alarming speed. Significant opportunities can be squandered without rapid decisions and timely action. Relying solely on the standard governance techniques described in chapter 4 is a good start, but it's not enough.

In addition to profiling the leader's management characteristics, there are seven actions a board that's gifted with a visionary should take on a regular basis.

1. ***Close the door:*** Executive sessions with the CEO out of the room are essential. The SEC mandates these closed-door meetings, but they take on critical importance in a brilliant-jerk

scenario. Executive sessions are the times when the board grapples with if, when, and how to get involved. It's not that boards with trailblazing CEOs don't do this, but not many do it well.

For real impact, the executive session agenda includes updates on the CEO's personality and work style, an honest appraisal of board performance to date, and the exploration of ideas to improve and better manage the relationship between the board and the pathfinder. One person who helped govern several rambunctious trailblazers told us, "The sessions create opportunity to improve performance and become more aware of their working relationship with the CEO. The sessions allow the board the opportunity to think, plan, and build their approach. They should ask what type of personality their leader has, acknowledge the strengths and weaknesses, and develop a plan to deal with it." Another person with hard-won experience described it as the time to discuss "what keeps you up at night." Staying on top of what needs to be done helps avoid meltdowns like we saw at Uber.

2. *Mind the gaps:* One of the most important functions of the board is supplementing the change maker's managerial gaps. A board needs to recruit members who bring relevant skills, experience, and perspective. Some

dominant visionaries start their company in their teens or early twenties with an innovative idea and little or no business knowledge or leadership experience. Larry Page at Google and Elizabeth Holmes at Theranos were youngsters when they started their companies. Whether the founder is young and inexperienced like those two or their career path has not given them exposure to key functions, the board has the responsibility to provide guidance to the CEO on how to supplement their leadership toolbox or find a senior executive that can join and balance out the leadership role like Schmidt did at Google. As a board member, your failure to act on this can significantly diminish growth.

3. ***Specialize:*** Governing a mercurial CEO requires special handling. For instance, executives could report directly to the board, such as the COO or CFO. Banks do something similar and have the chief risk officer report to the risk committee. Like banks that have a special committee for risk, if you're responsible for governing a pioneering CEO, you need a committee focused on supporting and governing the imaginative leader. A board member of a tech leader in Silicon Valley recalled that a former CEO from another company added important experience and gravitas to this specialized board role—basically another version of an adult in the room. Likewise,

when Kenneth I. Chenault retired as chief executive of American Express and joined the board of Airbnb, he added much-needed experience and the ability to help the board assist cofounder Brian Chesky.

4. *Curate the culture:* If "culture eats strategy for breakfast," why do some boards pay so much more attention to strategic oversight? While the boards were looking at strategic issues, cultural erosions at VW and Uber were not detected early enough, and destructive behaviors spread throughout the company. To give culture the attention it deserves, boards establish a committee to actively oversee goals, incentives, practices, and processes that drive behaviors and the company culture. This committee regularly monitors and audits the company culture, ethics, adherence to a code of conduct, and the dominant visionary's relationship with others. They get a good handle on the cultural evolution and company values by tapping into employees, hotline and whistleblower reports, and HR because, as the Netflix Culture document says, "The actual company values, as opposed to the nice-sounding values, are shown by who gets rewarded, promoted, or let go."

5. *Be contrarian:* The CEO's brilliance generates the electricity that energizes a company's success, but not everyone can be right all the time. A former board director said even the best like

Jobs only had "one good idea out of ten." The exact ratio of good to bad ideas varies with each disrupter, but realize that not all their ideas are great. Challenging the ingenious leader and keeping them focused is one of the board's most important jobs.

Contrary opinions are essential to spark constructive conversations and make smarter judgments. Boards are wise to avoid getting involved in the nitty-gritty business decisions. But when there are big bets to be made with large potential risks and rewards, developing rigorous questions and different approaches is a smart investment. Though the board may decide to follow the founder's lead, it is prudent to independently evaluate options. "Often the board does not act sufficiently suspicious. Only a small percentage of directors are good at pushing back. They tend to trust the CEO too much" was the observation of a seasoned member of the board. "Board members tend to want to please the CEO. That creates a conflict with their duty. Their job is to poke holes and ask tough questions."

Airing alternate viewpoints and encouraging constructive conversations produce results. Apple's board regularly aired "strong differing opinions" and alternate viewpoints on key strategic and investment decisions. Several companies use red-blue team exercises to aggressively debate significant issues and potential changes in strategy and execution from two different points of view. Other firms include external experts to develop contrary opinions void of internal biases to fully vet the proposals.

You and your board need to realize that some discussions can be difficult. We have witnessed firsthand how discussions between senior executives or board members and dominant visionaries are often fraught with challenges. One board member we worked with heard rumors that company engineers, product developers, and marketers were convinced that a major new company offering would not succeed. Some thought that the engineering was not fully developed and tested, and others were convinced that the products would be rejected by the market. And everyone was afraid to tell the boss because he hated any sort of challenge.

Nonetheless, the board member broached the subject with the imperious CEO, who said these employees lacked vision. The executive was confident that this new offering would succeed. He emphasized that he was the founder and largest shareholder, that she should forget about the issue and not worry about it, and she should certainly not talk to the employees about it—or alarm the other board members. What should the board member do? Should she talk to the concerned employees over the

CEO's objection? Was this important enough to bring to the board's attention?

With some coaching, she decided it was her responsibility to get more information and report it to the board. She gathered the facts and, with support of other members, made the case to the CEO that the board had the responsibility to be thorough and rigorous in evaluating and possibly approving the expenditures for the new offering. The CEO was indignant. He did not appreciate that board member's talking directly to senior staff without his permission or what he viewed as unnecessary, burdensome, and costly oversight. But it did change the dynamics of the CEO's relationship with the board and over time improved the ability of the board to receive timely and valuable information and then to provide effective input to decisions.

We were cautioned by board members, and want to pass on to you, that whatever approach the board employs to spark discussions, it is essential to engage the board *early* in the exploration and decision analysis rather than confront the board late in the process. Waiting too long in the decision cycle stacks the deck in favor of the CEO's idea no matter how good or bad it is.

The best processes cannot totally avoid conflict. Boards should expect the visionary to dig in their heels periodically and reject advice because they are convinced their approach is correct. That brings us to the next two board actions.

6. ***Expect resistance:*** Sometimes the smartest person in the room needs someone to stop them from doing something dumb. Challenging a person who's on a mission to change the world is a tricky thing to do, especially when they have voting control. Conflicts sometimes flare up during a discussion of contrary opinions, and the CEO will refuse to back off their plan even if it is dangerously flawed. Power influences people. Over time, they become less risk aware, less adept at seeing things from other people's points of view.

   In advance of this sort of problem, the board and CEO should establish a civil and just way to resolve conflicts such as taking the issue off-line. Otherwise, the conflict becomes rancorous. Board members with a long history of dealing with dominant visionaries told us that if they believed the CEO was risking the company's well-being but would not back down, as a method of last resort they would threaten to resign and mean it. The threat of one or more resignations was usually enough to back down most, but not all, difficult bosses.

7. ***Build paths of least resistance:*** When major conflicts arise, one-on-one discussions are

almost always more productive than open discussion in the boardroom. Discussions of sensitive issues in front of the board can threaten the visionary and make them defensive. Coaching and private conversations are something you must include in your playbook. Someone that sat on the board of a tech company and dealt with a world-class domineering change maker (and sometimes jerk) told us private discussions were the only way he was able to get the CEO to change his mind on many contentious issues. Edgar S. Woolard, a board chair at Apple, coached Steve Jobs after he returned to head Apple a second time. They developed a warm relationship that blossomed outside of the boardroom. Not only did Woolard reach out to Jobs to work through issues one on one, Jobs, normally confident to rely on only his opinion, would call Woolard at home to get advice.

The core governing roles and practices of an active board are enough for most companies but not ones with a powerful leader bent on changing the world. The evaluation of your CEO and these seven governance keys will give you and the board what you need to ride the governance roller coaster and succeed.

KEYS TO GOVERNING A VISIONARY LEADER

Close the door—hold executive sessions that get to the heart of board involvement

Mind the gaps—fill in managerial holes in the CEO's repertoire of skills

Specialize—add structure and board resources to increase collaboration

Curate the culture—build board processes to monitor the company culture the CEO is creating

Be contrarian—make early discussion of alternatives standard practice

Expect resistance—build a process to handle disagreements and flare-ups before they happen

Build paths of least resistance—establish one-on-one channels between the board and CEO

INTERVENTION

Building a company around a charismatic founder makes sense. Investors, employees, and boards are drawn to a person who can create a robust new company and disrupt the status quo. Sometimes, things go smoothly, the company grows under the direction of the CEO, and the board works out of the spotlight.

Salesforce and Amazon boards have remained behind the scenes for years. You almost never hear about them.

Other times a provocative founder ends up in hot water, either through poor strategic decisions or behavior that angers employees, investors, and, in the case of Elon Musk, regulators. When that happens, the board gets active and visible. We saw the Uber board shift into action when it became apparent something had to be done to reverse public opinion. They pushed out Kalanick, the source of the trouble, and brought in "humble" and "no-nonsense" Dara Khosrowshahi to lead the company and shift the aggressive culture that had grown during Kalanick's leadership.

Sometimes, even when a board is diligent, conflicts arise, the relationship with the forward-thinking genius sours, and constructive conversations cease. It becomes a war zone of conflicting interests and power plays. Often, there is an exodus of senior executives. At the point where internal conflicts or external problems rage out of control, the board must seriously consider the nuclear option of removing the CEO. That's what happened with Steve Jobs and the Apple board in 1985. Uber and Apple are far from the only companies to wrestle with this issue. Clothing chain American Apparel tolerated years of controversy before dumping founder Dov Charney in 2014. And pizza chain Papa John's fired its troublesome founder John Schnatter in 2018. Firing the CEO is not something any board wants to do, but given the track record with firebrand mavericks, every board should be ready to act.

KEEPING IT REAL

The board's job is to help make the visionary CEO unstoppable, free from unnecessary constraints that would hinder the fulfillment of the next big mission. But the board members we talked to that have dealt with visionaries all agreed most boards do not have the tools they need.

Successful boards provide strategic oversight, have clarity on the important aspects of the business, and are rigorous in their coaching and questioning. That includes asking tough questions and poking holes in assumptions to improve both concept and execution. But they don't micromanage. The person leading the company is the only one who owns the innovative vision. It's their baby.

Three pieces combine to create a collaborative and active board—the best way to stay productive with and govern an unconventional leader. First, you need to put in place the basic building blocks of governance— accountability, senior level staffing and evaluation, and strategic oversight. Second, you need an active board with enhanced processes and improved criteria for membership and composition. To complete the set, you need to embrace all seven of the key ingredients and a tailored approach to collaboration. Combined properly, these three govern the unique opportunities and risks the temperamental trailblazer brings.

Board members and executives we talked to agree that the board should err on the side of not interfering with the visionary's quest to build a stupendous

CREATING A BETTER BOARD IF YOU DON'T HAVE A DOMINANT VISIONARY

The presence of a dominant visionary is an extreme case—one where the board's role may make the difference between glorious success or ignoble disaster. But every board should set aside time to evaluate how well they create and sustain value. Following are key questions you should ask:

- *Are we supporting the CEO to make and execute big bets? How can we do better?*

- *Is the board membership adequate to support the CEO's big bets? Are there processes in place and sufficient diversity to allow constructive conversations and avoid major mistakes?*

- *Does the board have a good handle on the CEO's management strengths and weaknesses?*

- *What does the leader need to do a better job? Are there resources that would fill gaps in their repertoire?*

- *Is all the information needed for constructive conversations and smart decisions available?*

- *Does the CEO know how to make the best use of the board?*

- *Are you sure you don't have a dominant visionary?*

- *Do you want someone in charge who can change the world?*

company. "Get their brilliant thoughts out in the open so the board can make something useful of it—and don't get in their way," was how one of our contacts put it. Amazon's board did a remarkable job in the early years of not second-guessing Bezos' unconventional business model and letting him run with it.

THREE EASY PIECES

While the board is being smart and staying out of the way, it has the ongoing responsibility to protect the long-term value of the company. We have described the board processes and activities that you can use to protect and enhance the value created. The nuclear option of removing the CEO—like we saw at Uber and Apple—is the board's last resort.

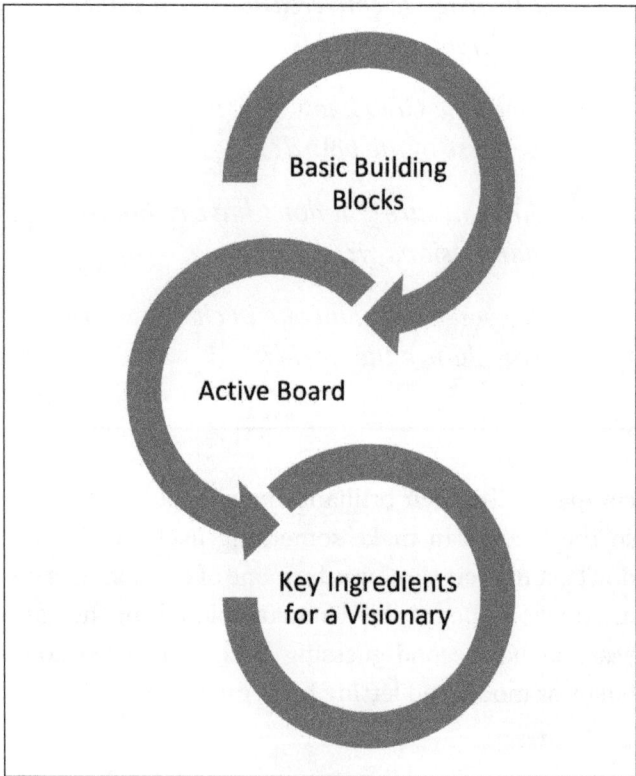

Basic Building Blocks

Active Board

Key Ingredients for a Visionary

CHAPTER 6

STRATEGIES FOR VCS, EXECUTIVES, EMPLOYEES, AND INVESTORS

The board is not the only one on stage with an audacious CEO. The other stakeholders—executives, employees, VCs, and other investors—have important roles to play. They have to provide stewardship for the organization in the face of the domineering CEO. Without a doubt, this can be a challenging proposition while asserting governance responsibilities to boot.

Many employees and most executives have nearly day-to-day contact with the chief executive. They have to manage and thrive in that environment. Sometimes, given a difficult taskmaster, that's not easy.

VCs and investors operate at more of a distance. They have infrequent interactions with the CEO, and some may only see the CEO at orchestrated events. Shareholder voice is an important part of the governance process. Even though shareholders work at a distance, when they speak up or get involved, it can put them in direct contact with the visionary leader.

VCs have another role if they sit on the board and will have more exposure to the CEO's operating style, including braininess and jerkiness.

We advise you to take to heart these recommendations.

VENTURE CAPITALISTS: MAKING THE MOST OF A CHALLENGING TALENT

If you are a venture capitalist, we want you to avoid a fiasco with your dominant visionary. To help you be successful and make sure you get healthy return on your investment, here are the mechanisms to steer your CEO in the right direction.

> *Lead the charge to implement best practices:* To deal with the range of opportunities and challenges a pioneering CEO with a strong personality provides, the board needs the most effective set of processes and practices. You are in a unique position to help. You can be the steward of best practices by bringing examples of what has worked to the board for

consideration and adoption. Given the portfolio of companies served, you have access to a wide range of board governance practices. Your experience, and the experience of your VC colleagues, provides insights and evaluations of alternate approaches.

Become the board member of choice: If you have been involved with the founder from the early days, you have special insight into the best and worst the CEO has to offer. That allows you to provide valuable advice and coaching to other members of the board. The longevity of your relationship may also allow preferred access. Cultivating a warm relationship allows you to be forthright with advice to the trailblazer—more than others involved in governance and coaching. Your relationship can also facilitate one-on-one discussions that help steer the CEO toward smarter decisions and away from corrosive behavior or disastrous actions. Your private conversations outside the boardroom can create important vectors for change.

Challenge board complacency: Activist boards produce the best results. They move much more quickly to help the CEO seize opportunities and sidestep problems. Your role is to periodically take a hard look at the adequacy of board activity. When you sense the board is drifting into a complacent valence, you can raise the issue with other board members to get their perspectives and then raise it for discussion with the entire board. It will make you a bit of a pain, but it is a vital role.

Be picky about the board composition: You of all people know the importance of board diversity. Use your network to find the very best candidates and get them interested and considered for board seats. Likewise, recruiting the best executives to support the top dog is a valuable role for you.

Consider starting a best practices playbook: You and your brethren VC see and hear more examples of what works and what doesn't than almost any board member. Capturing the lessons about how to best coach and govern brilliance, arrogance, jerkiness, and other traits of challenging leaders would be worth its weight in gold for the VC in your firm. Rather than a collection of sordid stories that named names and dished the dirt on flagrant actions, this would be a discreet and confidential guide to optimizing board performance.

EXECUTIVES: SPEAK TRUTH TO POWER

Your job as an executive is to face unbridled dominance, find the best path forward, and challenge proposed decisions on an almost daily basis. That can put you in harm's way. Here's how to not just avoid getting caught in the line of fire but make going to work every day more positive and productive.

Monitor the culture: You are in a perfect position to get a read on the company culture. Periodically assess what is going on—include data regarding incidents or problems as well as the extent to which people in the organization demonstrate the behaviors that characterize the values of the company. The informed perspective will be useful to you and your executive team and provide important information in conversations with the CEO and board.

Find a way to include board members in key executive meetings: One of the very best things you can do to give the board a sense of what is really going on in the company is to have them attend some of your executive meetings. They will see firsthand how decisions are made, who makes them, and the culture of the company in action. Netflix does this and it works well. But getting the CEO to agree to this sort of thing can be tricky, especially if they dominate decision-making. We have seen CEOs block all board access to executives. You will need to explore with great care ways to get the board to introduce this as a needed governance function.

Make sure board members have access to you: Executives can provide perspectives the board needs to do its job. But they have to have access to you. It's their job to make that happen, but you have to let them know you're available to help make the CEO a success. That includes having a balanced perspective and well-articulated ideas of how things are working and areas for improvement that would interest a board member. If you engage as just a naysayer or with a chip on your shoulder, your effectiveness is diminished.

Explore ways to enjoy the gain and relieve the pain: To thrive in an ecosystem with a dominant leader, an executive needs to find ways to enjoy the good times and get past the tough ones. You need to find a way to make that happen. We don't know what will work for you—different corporate cultures favor different approaches. Look around and see what works best in yours. It could be humor, a support or discussion group, or mentoring.

Be an early-warning system: As an executive, you receive signals that are useful indicators of trouble brewing or the evolution of strengths. Signals emanate from execs you know from other companies, headhunters, VCs, and investors. As part of your executive function, seek, gather, and analyze these resources so they can be used effectively by the CEO and board. You don't want hearsay or unsubstantiated rumors. Search for information from several valuable sources and add a perspective that can help make a difference in upcoming decisions.

Run hard or resign: If the conditions are mostly favorable, work to make the CEO successful. But if the company environment doesn't fit your comfort level, or the organization is headed for a CEO-led disaster, bail out. You don't want to be a *mugwump* straddling the fence between getting things done and naysaying the CEO. Having your *mug* hanging over one side of the fence with the CEO, and your *wump* hanging over the other is not good for you or the company. Be decisive and act. If you jump ship, your decision might even send a signal to executives and the board that change is required, especially if other executives resign.

We think you should embrace all six of these executive actions. We realize that embracing any one of these may seem extremely risky to you. But consider the options. The upside of taking the risk is the potential for better governance, a company that is more likely to succeed, and the fulfillment of your own resilience. Without these actions, a hard-driving maverick can make your life really tough. You could become traumatized, feel isolated as you see other executives leaving at a high rate, and begin worrying about the black mark on your résumé if the company craters. Taking action is the best bet.

EMPLOYEES: BE HEALTHY AND HEARD

You are on the front line and often see the problems first. You can raise your voice and draw attention to problems. Employees played important parts in the uncovering of fraud at Theranos and hastened the changing of the guard at Uber. On the other hand, your front-line position helps you identify the behaviors that make the company great. And if you let yourself get inspired by the company's performance or results, you can thrive in the environment the CEO creates no matter how demanding or challenging it becomes.

Here's what we recommend for employees so you can thrive, survive, and keep sane.

Create a badge of courage: You and the other employees should confer a badge of courage on those who have been verbally savaged by an insufferable boss—recognition that they have been through the wringer and come out alive to remain focused on the company goals. This acknowledgment reduces the stigma and establishes camaraderie among employees. Offering praise for staying professional despite the humiliation may also offer a positive rein-forcement that works as a salve on the wound. In one organization we supported, it was con-sidered an honor to have been the target of hostility by the leader. In the team's view, the target had been brave enough to speak up and smart enough to have something important to say. Apple employees reportedly used to vote on who Jobs treated the worst that year. The dubious achievement meant you were tough and somehow survived. Admittedly the badge of courage is a coping mechanism and not a solution, but it keeps spirits lifted. It works. Or you can do as Bob Sutton, leadership professor at Stanford University, suggests: pretend you're a specialist in jerks and think about how you're "really lucky to see this spectacular, amazing specimen."

Get noticed: Get permission to kick off a program or experience in which a few selected employees are invited to write a letter to the CEO, board, and executives. Participants from across the organization should be chosen for each memo. The authors offer advice, detail something they are most proud of, and identify an emerging problem area. The spirit of the letter is factual, specific, and constructive. The letter is designed to expose problems and opportunities that may not be visible from the top of the organization and provide a sense of the positive values and attitudes of the people. They are only snapshots, but the correspondence you create will establish a voice for employees and provide valuable insights not available elsewhere.

Speak up: You and the other employees need to be heard because you have so much at risk if things go bad and much to gain when the company succeeds. With a terror-inducing boss in the top position, you are often abused and always feel unsafe. You can even develop PTSD.

You know that if the company fails spectacularly, it can be a black mark on your résumé. Some of the Theranos employees have struggled to break free from the stigma. Some have found life after, but others have labored for months or years to get back in the employment pool. And many former Enron employees faced the same challenges after the company imploded. We don't want that to happen to you.

When you do speak, don't just be a naysayer that harps on the negatives—speak up about the things that are right and contribute to the company's success. That makes you credible and keeps you from being a jerk.

Become a valuable barometer for executives: Executives have a voice, and you can provide them with indispensable input. You need to let them know you are available and have perspectives to help them do their job of making the boss a success. Figure out what executives need for a balanced perspective of how things are working and find a way to get that information to them. Working with a group rather than going solo may be a far better way for you to convey the message. Employees at Google banded together and amassed more than a thousand signatures to challenge the credibility of some of the committee members of an AI ethics council Google had formed. The committee was abandoned a week later. The biggest display of organized dissatisfaction happened when twenty thousand Googlers walked out to protest the company's handling of sexual harassment allegations against executives.

Be all in or get out: You need to find ways to make the leader's groundbreaking plans and brainy ideas come to life. They can't succeed without your committed execution. That not only means you have to work, it requires you to up your game. Spectacular results are unlikely to come from pedestrian execution. You will have to find ways to get beyond the tough environment and jerky behaviors. If you can't operate at a higher level than usual and find ways to mitigate the environmental friction generated by a demanding CEO, realize that former US president Harry S. Truman was right—*If you can't stand the heat, get out of the kitchen.* It's possible that you are not cut out for the job or that the environment is too corrosive. Either way, your exit is the best way forward.

THE IMPORTANCE FOR ALL STAKEHOLDERS TO SPEAK UP

There is solace in knowing you are not alone. Constructive conversations (which are not the same as bitch sessions) can cement the resolve to speak up among all interested parties. Stakeholders are often in the best position to see issues in the early stages and to help nip potential problems in the bud.

It is common for people to hesitate to share an observation or experience. They are unsure how acceptable their view is and stay silent. This phenomenon is widespread and occurs among all manner of senior executives, VCs, and corporate boards, and is even more common when the companies are controlled by a headstrong maverick.

We were advisers to a corporate board led by a dominant visionary when one board member told us that a senior executive confided he had significant concerns about the soundness of some of the CEO's proposed actions. The senior executive was reluctant to share his doubts with other executives because he was unsure whether others felt similarly and he did not want to be seen as a troublemaker.

The board member was in a quandary. He hesitated to share the information with other board members or the CEO because of the likely disruption it could cause to board dynamics and the relationship with the chief executive. And if he revealed the source of his information, the senior executive's position could be in jeopardy.

We encouraged our client to share concerns with others on the board in a confidential setting, without the CEO present. In that way, he could determine the board's assessment of the information. We also encouraged him to uncover whether others had similar reservations. As it happened, the discussion revealed that multiple members of the board had comparable concerns. That gave the client confidence to raise the issue to the CEO privately. The CEO was unhappy with the concerns being raised and probably would have dismissed them if only one person had voiced them, but hearing that these were concerns of executives and that numerous board members were in alignment, the CEO responded with changes to his proposed actions.

As board members have concerns, or hear about issues from other stakeholders, it is their responsibility to voice those misgivings and bring them to the board's attention to fulfill their responsibility for strategic oversight and accountability. But the responsibility to speak up extends all the way to executives and employees.

"As far as lessons learned from Theranos, I would say transparency is probably the biggest thing," said Tyler Shultz, an employee at Theranos who disclosed the fraud. He said that if he were starting a new company and there was a problem, "I would want any of my employees to tell me immediately without hesitation, and that was not the case at Theranos. The biggest thing is being aware of problems."

INVESTORS: ONLY ONE TASK

You, as investors, are vital stakeholders. But many investors don't get involved. They are willing to bet their money on the brilliance of a CEO to create a successful company and change an industry, but their involvement stops there. They sit back and watch.

Are you one of the investors who values a good story from a charismatic genius over prudent oversight? Once you invest your money, do you engage and genuinely get involved, or do you step back and fall out of touch?

If you fall into that trap, you could find yourself frequently mystified, sometimes horrified, and probably vulnerable to nightmares about losing your investment. If things go badly, your only resort may be a lawsuit and psychiatric counseling. But in the end, you'll only have yourself to blame and never recover your investment.

Consider this: What would it take for you to get involved? How would you want to be sure you get a return on your investment—especially when there's a live wire driving the creative, barely controlled chaos? You may be tempted to go with the flow, roll with it, stay passive. But remember, the stakes are high.

There is one thing, and only one thing, for you to do when a brainy CEO is leading the charge: be an active investor. Demand the best from the entire team—the board, CEO, executives, and employees. Hold everyone accountable.

That includes yourself. Don't bet on the story the CEO spins, watch for early gains, and then sit back. Be smart and vocal from the beginning about the structure of the board and the need for leading governance practices. Demand well-analyzed, credible data. Applaud brilliance in the CEO, board, and executives, when the merits are evident. And to borrow a phrase from diplomacy, trust but verify.

PUBLIC: AN OVERLOOKED ROLE

The general public is usually the audience that witnesses the drama of a brainy jerk rather than a stakeholder with a role in the play. When things go well and a leader's genius turns into a success story, the thrilled and awed public applauds the performance. That's what happened with Steve Jobs 2.0. Movies were made, and there are still articles being published about his larger-than-life accomplishments. But when things go topsy-turvy, like they did at Enron and Uber, the public is mystified and even horrified at how wrong things can go. The bad CEO becomes a media sensation for the public.

The story of Elizabeth Holmes and the Theranos debacle has become the subject of a book, countless articles, a televised documentary, and a movie. The shenanigans of Elon Musk consistently generate articles and lots of attention. The public eats up these stories even though they are not stakeholders and are usually not affected.

We believe the public needs more than the drama. People should receive information to help them see clearly what is really going on—and why. They need to know how these visionaries end up in positions of power, what traits they possess that make them so disarming and difficult, and what boards, executives, and employees can do to make them successful. The vox populi has power. People need to make their voices heard.

Just as journalism serves as the fourth estate—a check and balance of the government—an informed business citizenry must pay attention to the workings of a healthy economy. We need an informed public that sees more than just a tech-titan drama and speaks with authority about the boundaries of good governance.

CHAPTER 7

ALL TOGETHER NOW

We have ample evidence that the complacency of a corporate board, paired with a brainy and stubborn nonconformist leader, presents a precarious scenario. These special bosses are different from most people. They are rule breakers and forces of disruption who don't hew to normal ways of thinking and acting. And it is never clear at the onset what kind of leader they will be or what they will do. They might create a robust company that disrupts the status quo in business. That's what people hope for and why they invest. Or, without warning, the genius might start acting like a jerk, alienate customers and employees, and threaten the well-being of their company. That makes them hard to understand and profitably coexist with, much less govern. In some cases, they join the dark side, commit fraud, and take their company down with them. And sometimes they overachieve and do all three.

AVOIDING A BIG MISTAKE

At this point you may have a sense that living with and governing a brainy CEO with a vision to challenge the status quo consists primarily of monitoring and constraining their bad behaviors so they don't screw up. That is only half true. The other half is what the board should not do.

Boards with an ingenious disrupter as CEO do not lead. Their job is to collaborate to make the CEO and company successful—to help them do good and avoid doing harm.

One of the best examples of how not to collaborate with a visionary occurred in 1962 with Leonard Bernstein, Brahms' Piano Concerto no. 1 in D Minor, and Canadian soloist Glenn Gould. Gould was a young, world-renowned, innovative pianist and a recognized musical genius. His playing was distinguished by remarkable technical proficiency and nuanced interpretation that challenged performance norms. Bernstein, a prodigiously talented and experienced musician, was the conductor of the New York Philharmonic Orchestra. The Brahms concerto is one of the most frequently performed in the world.

The two players in this concerto—the soloist and the orchestra—work in collaboration. The soloist is front and center; they lead, and the orchestra follows. But it is not a one-sided relationship. The orchestra plays an important role, musically conversing back and forth with the soloist, nuancing and adding to the soloist's performance. They collaboratively execute, with the soloist leading the charge.

The word *concerto* comes from Italian. The exact etymology is uncertain but appears to be the fusion of two Latin words—*conserere*, meaning to tie, join, or weave together; and *certamen*, to fight or be in competition. We use the term *in concert* to mean working together. The dual meaning describes exactly what a concerto has been for the past four centuries—a sophisticated tussle between the dominant soloist and the supporting orchestra.

Before Gould took the stage to play the Brahms concerto, Bernstein made one of the most controversial announcements in musical performance history.

> You are about to hear a rather, shall we say, unorthodox performance of the Brahms D Minor Concerto, a performance distinctly different from any I've ever heard, or even dreamt of for that matter, in its remarkably broad tempi and its frequent departures from Brahms' dynamic indications. I cannot say I am in total agreement with Mr. Gould's conception.

Orchestra leaders at a concerto have always remained silent and let the spotlight shine on the soloist. Not Bernstein. While he acknowledged Gould's innovative approach, Bernstein slammed Gould, saying he did not agree with Gould's concept of how it should be played. Everyone was aghast. But Bernstein did not stop there. Next, he raised the question of who was in charge.

> But the age-old question remains: "In a concerto, who is the boss; the soloist or the conductor?" The answer is, of course, sometimes one, sometimes the other, depending on the people involved. But almost always, the two manage to get together by persuasion or charm or even threats to achieve a unified performance.
>
> But this time the discrepancies between our views are so great that I feel I must make this small disclaimer.

Bernstein said there was a question of who was in charge. Not really; at least for this concerto, that argument was settled long ago in the soloist's favor. Everyone could see Bernstein was challenging Gould and preemptively taking control of the performance.

Bernstein applauded Gould's artistry and noted "moments of freshness" in his interpretation—a clear case of damning with faint praise. Before he finished his remarks, to make his displeasure clear, Bernstein called Gould's interpretation a "wholly new and incompatible concept." No one could believe their ears.

Bernstein destroyed any hope of the "unified performance" when he stepped out of his supporting role and publicly challenged Gould's innovation and leadership. The worst offense was that he said in public what should have been said only in private. Conceivably Bernstein might have shared some or all of his views with Gould as part of a collaborative conversation. And he might have confided in private with the inner circle of orchestra funders and stakeholders. But a public announcement was over the top and destructive.

Being critiqued and undercut in public was too much for Gould to bear. He was stung by the affront and not long after gave up playing in public.

The soloist's leadership of the Brahms concerto in collaboration with the conductor and orchestra has a very strong resemblance to the modalities of a dominant visionary, the lead board director, and the board.

ROLES AND COMMON CHARACTERISTICS

BRAHMS CONCERTO	ROLES AND COMMON CHARACTERISTICS	COMPANY WITH A DOMINANT VISIONARY
Soloist	Establishes the way things will be done and leads execution	CEO
Orchestra conductor	Ensures successful collaboration	Lead board director
Orchestra	Supports, collaborates, and takes the lead on occasion	Board and executive team

The lessons for a board, executives, employees, and investors from the Bernstein episode are clear. First and foremost, the soloist is in charge and supported by the lead director and orchestra to execute the vision. Trying to reverse roles violates the very nature of the endeavor. The same is true of the CEO's mandate to execute their vision and the board and stakeholders' responsibility to support them.

Second, there is an inherent creative tension and back-and-forth between the soloist and the conductor and orchestra. Their collaboration explores and extracts value from different points of view of the approach and execution. Bernstein had it exactly right about leadership when he said, "Almost always, the two manage to get together by persuasion or charm or even threats to achieve a unified performance." That pretty much describes a brilliant CEO and their board having a way to discuss options, reconcile differences, and move forward to harness the strengths of both parties.

Third, an inventive rule breaker should be able to tolerate contrary points of view. But board members with years of experience tell us visionary leaders typically don't handle public confrontation well. They get defensive and sometimes petulant. Private conversations are usually the best way to proceed. Direct confrontation creates disharmony and undermines collaboration. Bernstein violated this rule. He chose a public forum for what should have been a private conversation, challenged the leader's role, and, rather than fuel a lasting partnership, hastened the retreat of genius.

MAKING IT WORK

Over the past ten years, we have been witnessing a Cambrian explosion of start-ups, a burst of radical change aimed at upending existing business models. Every day investors foie gras start-ups with cash to drive growth of disruptive business models. As a result, boards, VCs, and investors are recruiting wizards at an increasing rate to lead the charge. The lure of a gifted trailblazer with the ability to create a powerhouse company that challenges the status quo is a magnetic draw for investors and employees. We are likely to see a steady stream of charismatic powerhouses put in the driver's seat.

Letting a brainy disrupter-in-chief lead without jeopardizing the company is a challenge. The worst approach you can use is to let them proceed unmonitored and unguided. They can't do everything to achieve the vision on their own; they may get into deep trouble if left unattended.

The second worst way you can proceed is to weaponize the board, make governance restrictive, and get in the CEO's way. The board supports, coaches, and keeps a watchful eye out to make sure things are going well. They are not the leader. That is, unless the visionary CEO really screws up. Then the board assumes the lead. But their role is to make sure that never happens.

The best visionary-led companies have a collaborative give-and-take between the CEO, board, and executive team. In many cases, the employees join in. Together, they establish and monitor norms for ethics and culture. Most importantly, the board and visionary are held to exceptionally high standards for performance. The brilliant boss's job is to create a highly valuable, robust, and sustainable company for all stakeholders. As a board member, executive, employee, or investor, your performance is judged on how well you help make that happen.

So, let's set the record straight. Brainy, maverick CEOs and their boards and executive teams need each other. Collaboration is essential to make the right decisions and provide just enough oversight to avoid actions that harm the company.

Dominant visionaries need to be left alone sometimes so they can do what they do best—see a better way to do things and make it a reality. To know when and how to get involved and when to stay away requires more than a cursory understanding of what makes the trailblazer tick. You need to understand what they know, what they don't, and their temperament and ethical compass. There is no single formula for governing and living with their brilliance; your approach must be crafted specifically for the maverick you've been gifted. Or the one you've embraced.

Many people and much of the media think genius leaders are a problem. They point to the headline-grabbing jerks and frauds. There is a problem, but it is not that we have brainy jerks and change makers in charge. It's how we govern and collaborate with them. Too few know how to make that happen—to collaborate and govern a visionary to get a great company that does good and avoids harming stakeholders.

Today the pressures for fast growth and value creation are intense—much more so than twenty years ago. Iconoclastic leaders are pulled in because they can accomplish more, faster. Asked about how well-prepared boards are to govern a strong visionary leader in this accelerated environment, a former CEO and Silicon Valley director replied, "Not enough."

The guidance in this book, based on understanding brainy, nonconformist CEOs and the gathered wisdom of board directors, executives, and employees that have dealt with dominant visionaries, is meant to help you change that.

ACKNOWLEDGMENTS

We thank the board members, CEOs, executives, employees, and investors who contributed their perspectives in making this book.

ABOUT THE AUTHORS

Marc J. Epstein was, until recently, Distinguished Research Professor of Management at Jones Graduate School of Business at Rice University in Houston, Texas. Prior to joining Rice, Dr. Epstein was a professor at Stanford Graduate School of Business, Harvard Business School, and INSEAD (European Institute of Business Administration).

With extensive academic research and practical experience in the implementation of corporate strategies and the development of performance metrics for use in them, Marc is considered one of the global leaders in the areas of innovation, governance, performance measurement, and accountability in both corporations and not-for-profit organizations.

Marc has written extensively on corporate and nonprofit board governance, the role of boards of directors, organizational trust, and corporate accountability. He is the author of twenty books and well over two hundred professional papers that have won numerous top academic, professional, and business awards. He also provides seminars, executive courses, consulting, and presentations to senior managerial audiences throughout the world.

Rob Shelton is a globally recognized Silicon Valley–based consultant, author, and speaker on entrepreneurial excellence, breakthrough innovation, and scaling to drive rapid growth. Over the past forty years, Rob served as a trusted partner and adviser to CEOs and senior executives at leading organizations in the valley and around the world. He led the innovation practice at PwC and was also founder of PwC's Global Financial Service Innovation Center. Rob was a speaker at the 2013 World Economic Forum's Summer Davos, and his work has been highlighted in *Bloomberg Businessweek*, the *Wall Street Journal*, *Forbes*, *Forbes Japan*, *Financial Times*, *strategy+business*, *CNN Financial News*, *Fast Company*, and on Bloomberg Radio and NPR.

Marc and Rob previously collaborated (also with Tony Davila) on *Making Innovation Work: How to Manage It, Measure It, and Profit from It* (2006), a bestselling book from Wharton School Publishing.

www.ingramcontent.com/pod-product-compliance
Lightning Source LLC
Chambersburg PA
CBHW031414180326
41458CB00002B/355